Fred Bacon

History of the second pilgrimage to Richmond

May, 1881

Fred Bacon

History of the second pilgrimage to Richmond
May, 1881

ISBN/EAN: 9783337283513

Printed in Europe, USA, Canada, Australia, Japan

Cover: Foto ©ninafisch / pixelio.de

More available books at **www.hansebooks.com**

HISTORY

OF THE

SECOND PILGRIMAGE

TO

RICHMOND,

BY

THE KNIGHTS TEMPLARS

OF

MASSACHUSETTS AND RHODE ISLAND

MAY, 1881.

COMPILED AND EDITED BY

FRED P. BACON,

STAFF CORRESPONDENT, BOSTON HERALD.

BOSTON:
PRINTED BY AUTHORITY OF DE MOLAY COMMANDERY.
1882.

BOSTON, October 26, 1881.

At the regular conclave of De Molay Commandery, held in Masonic Temple, October 26, 1881, it was unanimously voted that a Committee, consisting of Sirs John W. Dadmun, Daniel F. Knight, J. M. Russell, George T. Ambrose and George F. Wright, be authorized to publish in book form a complete history of the Second Pilgrimage of De Molay Commandery to Richmond, Va., and that they be authorized to employ Fred P. Bacon, of the *Boston Herald*, who accompanied the Commandery as correspondent of that paper, as editor.

GEO. PHIPPEN, JR.,
Recorder.

CONTENTS.

	PAGE
INTRODUCTION,	7

THE START, ... 16

   LEAVING THE HUB IN A RAIN STORM.—THE NIGHT ON THE SOUND.—A SAFE AND SPEEDY RUN TO WASHINGTON.—THE ROSTER OF THE COMMANDERY AND FULL LIST OF THE PILGRIMS.

IN WASHINGTON, ... 21

   A CORDIAL RECEPTION.—SOCIAL COURTESIES EXTENDED.—VISIT TO MOUNT VERNON.—A RECEPTION AT THE WHITE HOUSE.—A CARRIAGE DRIVE ABOUT THE CITY.

IN FREDERICKSBURG, ... 31

   A GENUINE SOUTHERN WELCOME.—THE PARADE AND ITS CHARACTERISTICS.—THE LADIES VIE WITH THE SIR KNIGHTS IN THE HOSPITALITIES EXTENDED.

AT RICHMOND, ... 37

   THE FORMAL RECEPTION.—THE ENTIRE CITY JOINS IN THE WELCOME.—THE ENTRANCE AMID BOOMING CANNON AND CHEERS.—THE VISITORS FEASTED AND FETED FOR FOUR DAYS.

IN BALTIMORE, ... 85

   THE MONUMENTAL CITY GIVES A HEARTY GREETING TO THE PILGRIMS.—AN EVENING RECEPTION AND BANQUET BY BEAUSEANT COMMANDERY.—A SHORT BUT ENJOYABLE VISIT.

	PAGE
THE NEW YORK RECEPTION, ...	94

PALESTINE COMMANDERY OFFERS SHELTER TO THE PILGRIMS. — A LUNCH AT MASONIC HALL. — AN ENTHUSIASTIC GREETING. — THE STREET PARADE. — OFF FOR BOSTON.

THE HOME RECEPTION, ...	101

THE BOSTON COMMANDERY EXTENDS A CORDIAL GREETING. — A STREET PARADE AND BANQUET. — THE WELCOME SPEECHES AND CONGRATULATIONS. — THE DE MOLAYS DISMISSED.

APPENDIX, ...	109

INTRODUCTION.

THE second pilgrimage of the Knights Templars of Massachusetts and Rhode Island to Richmond, calls for the addition of another volume to the history of the friendly relations between the Sir Knights of New England and Virginia. The interchange of visits between the De Molay and St. John's and the Richmond Commanderies has been a notable illustration of the strength of the tie which binds together the Order throughout the Christian world, for the hearty good-will which has been shown in all the intercourse between the "two colonies of Virginia" has not been interrupted even by the sad events of the war. A brief resumé of the visits exchanged by the Commanderies of the two sections of the country will best introduce the events of the second pilgrimage of the De Molay and St. John's Commands. An invitation was extended in the year 1858 by the De Molay Commandery, of Boston, to the Richmond Commandery, No. 2, of Richmond, Virginia, to visit Boston and participate in the celebration of St. John's Day of that year, and in response to the invitation, the Richmond Sir Knights arrived in Boston, Thursday, June 23, 1858, to take part in the events of the following day. In addition to the parade on Friday, the visiting Commandery were hospitably entertained in Boston until Saturday evening, and the St. John's Commandery, of Providence, extended courtesies to the Richmond Sir Knights upon their arrival and departure from that city *en route*. Upon reaching home, the Richmond Commandery passed a series of resolutions acknowledging the courtesies extended during the visit to Boston, and concluding with the statement:

"We consider De Molay Commandery *pledged* to return our visit, either on May 13, June 24, or at any time during the year 1859 that may suit their convenience."

In February, 1859, correspondence between the two Commands resulted in an arrangement for a return visit of the De Molays in the following May, the events of which have already been duly recorded in a permanent form. Early in the year 1875, when the plans for the celebration of the Centennial of the Battle of Bunker Hill were under discussion, it was decided by the De Molay Commandery to invite the Richmond Commandery to take part in the Masonic parade on that occasion, and renew the acquaintances so long interrupted by the strife of the civil war. Under date of March 31, 1875, a cordial letter of invitation was sent by the De Molay Commandery to Richmond, asking the Fraters of Virginia to come to Massachusetts and allow an opportunity for a return of the generous hospitality extended to the Sir Knights of De Molay and St. John's Commands in 1859. The invitation was accepted by the Richmond Commandery, under date of April 8, 1875, and on Wednesday afternoon, June 16, 1875, the Knights Templars of Boston and vicinity turned out with full ranks and received their Virginia brethren and escorted them to Faneuil Hall, where the city officials welcomed the Southern guests. On the following day the Richmond Knights took part in the great parade and an excursion down the harbor, on Friday they enjoyed a carriage drive through the suburbs, and a banquet on Saturday concluded the festivities of the visit. On Sunday the Sir Knights attended the services at Music Hall, which were led by Rev. W. H. H. Murray, and at 7.30 on Monday morning took the train for Providence. All the courtesies possible to the limited stay of the Virginians in Providence were extended by the Sir Knights of that city. The visit was a fitting part of the long history of friendly intercourse between the Commanderies of the "two colonies of Virginia," and the Richmond guests did not depart for their homes without a promise from their Northern brethren that they should again welcome the De Molays and St. John's to the hospitalities of Richmond. It was in February, 1881, that this promise was recalled to the minds of the De Molay Commandery by the receipt of the following letter:

RICHMOND, VA., 4th Feb., 1881.

The Members of Richmond Commandery and The Commandery of St. Andrew to the Members of De Molay Commandery, of Boston, and of St. John's Commandery, of Providence.

GREETING:

For the purposes of cementing closer and stronger the bonds of knightly fellowship and love which have for so many years existed and be continued between us, we desire again to have you under our vine and fig tree. We therefore extend to you a cordial and knightly invitation to visit us in the City of Richmond, at such period during the year of 1881 as may best comport with your pleasure, comfort and convenience. The undersigned, a committee, feel honored in being made a medium to convey to their loved Fraters the invitation, and they give expression to the fondly cherished hopes of the members of their Commanderies that the invitation will be accepted by you as cheerfully, heartily and affectionately as it is extended, and then they will feel assured that its purpose will be accomplished.

We are, in bonds of knightly friendship and love,
   Yours most truly,
     WILLIAM B. ISAACS, *Chairman.*
     W. T. ALLEN.
     THOS. J. EVANS.
     JAMES A. SCOTT.
     WM. E. TANNER.
     LUCIEN L. BASS.

This invitation was formally accepted by vote of the De Molay Commandery, and a general committee of twenty-seven was appointed for the duty of making all the arrangements needed for a visit of the Commandery to Richmond in May. The general committee was composed of the following:

COUNCIL.

F. G. WALBRIDGE, *Eminent Commander.*
H. P. HEMENWAY, *Generalissimo.*
GEORGE F. WRIGHT, *Captain General.*

GENERAL COMMITTEE.

P. E. Sir Rev. J. W. DADMUN,	Sir S. A. TRIPP,
P. E. Sir M. WILLIAMS,	Sir C. B. BARRETT,
P. E. Sir JOHN M. CLARK,	Sir G. S. CLARK,
P. E. Sir C. B. LANCASTER,	Sir J. H. COLLINS,
P. E. Sir J. B. MASON,	Sir P. E. DOLLIVER,
Sir JOHN MACK,	Sir A. F. NETTLETON,
Sir J. W. FAIRBANKS,	Sir D. F. KNIGHT,
Sir B. F. GUILD,	Sir E. B. HOLMES,
Sir S. D. NICKERSON,	Sir WM. B. FISHER,
Sir J. M. RUSSELL,	Sir F. L. PARKER,
Sir F. W. SMITH,	Sir G. S. CARPENTER,
Sir J. O. WETHERBEE,	Sir G. PHIPPEN, Jr.

The transportation committee, consisting of Sir Knights William B. Fisher and F. L. Parker, visited Richmond in April to make arrangements for the trip, and received a most cordial welcome from the members of the Richmond Commanderies. At an entertainment given the De Molay committee, by the invitation committee of the

Richmond Commanderies, the following verses were read by Sir Knight Thomas J. Evans, of the Richmond committee:

> We live in the South, where the sun rules the day,
> A pillar of beauty, effulgent each ray;
> A halo of glory encircles his brow —
> At his rising and setting the earth makes a bow.
>
> We live in the land where the mocking bird sings,
> And the butterfly spreads to the sun her bright wings;
> Where the peach blossom opens its beautiful eyes
> Ere the Spring-time has come or Old Winter dies;
> Where in forests the fragrant magnolia grows,
> The cactus, pomegranate, the orange, the rose;
> Where the melon is perfect in flavor and size,
> A charm to the taste, a delight to the eyes;
> Where the small foot of woman treads lightly the earth,
> Giving proof of her breeding and excellent birth;
> Where men are as proud as the proudest of kings,
> And many as poor as the poorest of things,
> Yet ready to share the last crumb with a friend,
> And stand by his side in a fight to the end.
>
> > We saw a lamb the other day,
> > Skipping o'er the lawn in play,
> > And it did gently, meekly say:
> > "Quarter me for De Molay."
>
> > Upon a tree, not far away,
> > There sat a bird — it was the jay;
> > We listened, and we heard him say:
> > "I will sing for De Molay."
>
> > Close by the tree there ran a brook;
> > It had a merry, happy look,
> > And as it threw its snowy spray
> > Against a rock right in its way,
> > In sounds of music it did say:
> > "Here's a bath for De Molay."

INTRODUCTION.

Across the brook a horse did stray
Along a field well set with hay;
He turned and looked, and then did neigh,
By which he plainly meant to say:
"Saddle me for De Molay."

Beasts and birds and streams unite
In urging Richmond to invite
The Boston Knights to come and see
Virginia's hospitality.

We will not promise overmuch;
Such as we have, we'll give you such —
Will try to make you feel as free
As those who meet and do agree.

We'll take you to the outer lines,
And there you'll see the Seven Pines;
And then we'll show you, if you will,
The top of famous Malvern Hill,
And take a peep at Gaines's Mill.

We'll take you sailing on the Jeemes,
So crooked that it often seems,
In going to its mouth,
To be in doubt how to get out —
By east, west, north, or south.

Dutch Gap you must not fail to see —
It was commenced by General B.;
Projected for the ends of war,
Completed under peace and law.

We want you to come. Though humble our home,
Our tongues and hearts say to De Molay, come!
The Sir Knights of Richmond with emphasis say
They wait with impatience the long-looked-for day
When the Sir Knights of Boston shall be our guests
And we shall establish by unfailing tests

> That we still recollect with unspeakable joy
> How you every delicate art did employ
> To make us the happiest men in the world,
> When, six years ago, our banners unfurled
> Were cheered by the people of Boston.

It was in response to the invitation that the pilgrimage was made which is the subject of the following pages, and in the records here presented an attempt has been made to put in a permanent form some slight history of the many happy events resulting from the visit. It would be impossible to present a full account of all that occurred in the ten days' absence from Boston, for every Sir Knight who joined in the tour had experiences worthy of equal prominence, so that only what may be called official records are given here. While Richmond was the objective point of the pilgrimage, the visiting Sir Knights found hearty greetings at Washington, Fredericksburg, Baltimore and New York, and the interchange of courtesies at each of these cities were quite an important part of the visit. The high standing of the Order in all the cities in which the Sir Knights found "food and shelter" was most fully shown by the space given to the events of their pilgrimage by the local press, that sure and trustworthy mirror of the popular mind. All the addresses delivered were spread out in full by the papers of the day, and the careful and accurate reports presented by the representatives of the several journals deserve a generous recognition in these records. The presence of Mr. D. C. Hall and his band of musicians added largely to the pleasures of the trip, as they were always ready to contribute to the enjoyment of the pilgrims, and met the demands upon their services cheerfully and creditably. Notwithstanding all the fatigues of such an extended journey, which, however, were mitigated largely by the fair weather granted the Sir Knights almost throughout their tour, there was not a case of serious illness to any member of the pilgrims, and the De Molays were complimented upon their admirable bearing in all the parades of the pilgrimage. It may be then safely assumed that the result of this visit tended to the more firmly unite the "two colonies of Virginia," and to strengthen the bonds of knightly love between the pilgrims and their entertainers.

THE START.

LEAVING THE HUB IN A RAIN STORM.—THE NIGHT ON THE SOUND.—A SAFE AND SPEEDY RUN TO WASHINGTON.—THE ROSTER OF THE COMMANDERY AND FULL LIST OF THE PILGRIMS.

THE Sir Knights of the De Molay Commandery assembled at Masonic Temple early on Thursday afternoon, May 19, 1881, to prepare for the street parade to the Old Colony depot, from which point they were to take their departure to enter upon the long and pleasantly anticipated Richmond Pilgrimage. A more unpropitious day could hardly have been selected, for a steady rain poured down in such a persistent fashion that all hope of the parade had to be abandoned, and one by one the Sir Knights found their way to the railroad station. Here a large crowd had assembled to give a hearty farewell to the pilgrims, and all sorts of kindly messages and greetings were sent to the Richmond Sir Knights by those who found it impossible to join in the visit. The band engaged by the De Molays for the trip, Hall's Boston Brass, was present, under its leader, Mr. D. C. Hall, and enlivened the scene by playing a number of selections, winding up with the old song, "Carry me back to Old Virginny," the strains of which rang out as the start was made. An uneventful run was made to Fall River, where the St. John's Command, of Providence, joined the De Molays aboard the boat. The Providence Commandery was accompanied by the American Band, of that city, Mr. D. W. Reeves, leader, and after supper the two bands contributed a very enjoyable concert programme, for the entertainment of all on board. On arriving in New York, the weather was found still anything but agreeable, and the trip across to Jersey City was made in a drizzling rain. A pleasant event of the morning was the courtesy shown the ladies of the visiting Commands by a committee from the Palestine Commandery, of New York City, in the presentation to each lady of a beautiful hand bouquet, as they passed from the Fall River boat to take the transfer boat to Jersey City. Taking the special train provided by the Pennsylvania Central Railroad Company at Jersey City, a rapid and uneventful run was made to Washington, where the Commands arrived at three o'clock on Friday afternoon, more than an hour in advance of the schedule time. For convenience, the roster of the Boston Sir Knights, with the full list of the ladies accompanying them, is here presented, this list including not only those who started from Boston with the party, but all who subsequently joined it at the several points *en route*. The entire Command numbers three hundred and sixty members.

OFFICERS.

Fred. G. Walbridge, *Eminent Commander.*
H. P. Hemenway, *Generalissimo.*
George F. Wright, *Captain-General.*
Rev. J. W. Dadmun, *Prelate.*
Henry G. Jordan, *Senior Warden.*
Daniel F. Knight, *Acting Junior Warden.*
Joseph M. Russell, *Treasurer.*
Wm. B. Fisher, *Acting Recorder.*
E. A. Loud, *Standard Bearer.*
J. Frank Gammell, *Sword Bearer.*
Zacheus Holmes, *Warder.*
Chas. A. Drost,
E. W. Gilbert, } *Guards.*
Geo. S. Carpenter,
J. W. Fairbanks,
Peter E. Dolliver, } *Commandery Fund Committee.*
Joseph B. Mason,
George O. Townsend, *Armorer and Sentinel.*
Howard M. Dow, *Organist.*
Charles B. Lancaster, *Past Commander.*
Rev. W. S. Studley, *Past Prelate.*
Fred. P. Bacon, *Correspondent Boston Herald.*

SIR KNIGHTS.

Geo. T. Ambrose.	S. P. Bartlett.
E. M. Ames.	Langdon Baxter.
H. B. Arnold.	Geo. B. Brown.
T. D. Atwood.	J. Bryant.
A. B. Babcock.	Joseph R. Carr.
A. T. Bacon.	W. F. Chester.
H. C. Barnabee.	E. R. Cheney.

I. W. Chick.
D. S. Clark.
J. H. Collins.
W. R. Cooke.
Charles A. Cox.
J. H. Cummings.
F. J. Davis.
J. H. Davis.
Pierpont Edwards.
F. C. Fairbanks.
R. G. Ferguson.
H. N. Fisher.
John Foster.
E. R. Frost.
A. J. Gordon.
T. W. Gould.
C. D. V. Graves.
E. S. Hamlin.
S. J. Harrison.
T. S. Hittinger.
E. B. Holmes.
A. D. Holmes.
M. S. Holway.
Geo. M. Hosmer.
J. A. Johnson.
E. T. Kent.
Wm. A. Kidder.
E. W. Leavens.

Wm. Lumb.
John Mack.
E. T. McIntire.
Geo. H. Maynard.
E. A. Messinger.
S. Noyes, Jr.
G. W. Oliver.
C. H. Olmsted.
B. J. Parker.
F. L. Parker.
J. H. Peak.
Charles Pierce.
E. M. Platt.
W. H. H. Porter.
C. M. Proctor.
G. J. Raymond.
G. F. Sanderson.
J. M. Smith.
C. W. Smith.
J. P. Soule.
Henry Stumcke.
Thos. A. Taylor.
A. H. Timson.
A. D. Thompson.
D. S. Watson.
A. Webster.
Lyman W. Wheeler.

THE LADIES.

Mrs. Geo. B. Brown.
Mrs. W. F. Chester.
Mrs. W. R. Cooke.

Mrs. J. H. Cummings.
Miss J. M. Fisher.
Mrs. T. Warren Gould.

Mrs. H. P. Hemenway.
Mrs. E. B. Holmes.
Mrs. A. D. Holmes.
Mrs. H. G. Jordan.
Mrs. D. F. Knight.
Mrs. J. B. Mason.
Mrs. E. T. McIntire.

Mrs. B. J. Parker.
Mrs. J. M. Smith.
Mrs. F. G. Walbridge.
Mrs. D. S. Watson.
Mrs. L. W. Wheeler.
Mrs. George F. Wright.

THE COMMITTEES.

The committees of the De Molay Commandery having charge of the pilgrimage were as follows :

Executive Committee. — Eminent Commander Fred. G. Walbridge, Past Eminent Commander John M. Clark, Past Eminent Commander Charles B. Lancaster, Past Eminent Commander Joseph B. Mason, Sir Knight Benjamin F. Guild, Sir Knight J. Otis Wetherbee, Sir Knight J. W. Fairbanks.

Committee on Music.— Sir Knight Joseph M. Russell, Past Eminent Commander Marlborough Williams, Past Eminent Commander Joseph B. Mason.

Transportation Committee. — Past Eminent Commander Charles B. Lancaster, Sir Knights William B. Fisher and F. L. Parker.

Ladies' Committee. — Past Eminent Commander Joseph B. Mason, Sir Knights Zacheus Holmes and E. A. Messinger.

Baggage Committee.— Sir Knights James H. Collins and George O. Townsend.

Printing Committee.— Sir Knights Benjamin F. Guild, George F. Wright, George Phippen, Jr.

IN WASHINGTON.

A Cordial Reception.—Social Courtesies Extended.—Visit to Mount Vernon.—A Reception at the White House.—A Carriage Drive about the City.

SUCH an unheard of event as the arrival of an excursion party ahead of its schedule time was naturally unanticipated by the Washington Sir Knights, but a telegram informed them of the fact, and the annual parade of the Mounted De Molay Commandery of Washington was cut short, and the several Commands reached the Baltimore and Potomac Railroad Station about an hour after the train arrived, the time thus afforded the visitors giving ample opportunities for preparing for the reception and parade through the principal streets. After the usual interchange of courtesies between the Reception Committee of the Washington Commands and the visiting Sir Knights, the procession was formed as follows: De Molay Mounted Commandery, No. 4, ninety saddles, headed by a full corps of buglers, under command of Sir M. R. Thorpe, Eminent Commander; E. F. Lawson, Generalissimo, and C. L. Patten, Captain-General. Potomac Commandery, No. 3, thirty in number, headed by Donch's Band, Sir George E. Corson,

Eminent Commander ; Sir John Lynch, Generalissimo, and Sir Daniel Johnson, Captain-General. Columbia Commandery, No. 2, one hundred in number, Sir William H. Browne, Eminent Commander; Sir D. B. Ainger, Generalissimo, and Sir John Wilson, Captain-General. Washington Commandery, No. 1, seventy in number, headed by the Marine Band, Sir W. J. Stephenson, Eminent Commander; William G. Brock, Generalissimo, and Sir William G. Moore, Captain-General. St. John's Commandery, of Providence, R. I., sixty-four in number, headed by the American Brass Band, followed by De Molay Commandery, of Boston, Mass., eighty-six in number, headed by Hall's Brass Band. The rear of the procession was composed of carriages containing the lady visitors, under the escort of the Reception Committee. The magnificent caparisoned horses of the mounted Commandery and the splendid uniforms of the Sir Knights presented a gorgeous spectacle as the procession passed over the line of march.

The effect upon the minds of the visitors as they passed through the streets of the National Capital was curiously noticed by the writer. Coming from Northern cities, where the residents are familiar with all organizations contemplating a visit, and make an effort to give all such visitors a welcome, the utter quiet of the crowds which lined the streets was somewhat depressing. Only once on the line of march, which extended through many of the prominent streets and avenues, was there any signs of a recognition of the visiting Sir Knights, and that from Riggs House, from a party of Boston guests. The motley crowd of the real Southern Negro population, which turned out in honor of the guests, presented a new phase of American life to many of the Northern Sir Knights, and the antics caused among this class by the enlivening strains of the bands beggar all description. When the head of the line reached Seventeenth and I Streets, by instructions, the bands ceased playing, as they were nearing the Executive Mansion, on account of the sickness of Mrs. Garfield. At five P. M. the head of the column entered the President's grounds, to pass in review before the Chief Magistrate. A large crowd had assembled within the enclosure, but, to their credit be it said, not the least noise was made. The President, with Attorney-General MacVeagh by his side, took position between the centre columns that face the portico. Then the line marched in review, the officers saluting and the President returning the compliment. Proceeding from the White House, the Commands passed, *via* Fifteenth, F, Thirteenth streets and Pennsylvania avenue, to Willard's Hotel, where the visitors were left, and the Washington Templars returned to the temple and were dismissed.

After refreshing the outward and inner man, the visiting Commands formed in line shortly before nine o'clock, and marched to the Masonic

Hall, where the formal reception ceremonies were to occur, the ladies of the Massachusetts and Rhode Island Commands having preceded their Sir Knights in carriages, under escort of the efficient Ladies' Committee of the Washington Commanderies. After the New England Knights had filed into the hall and stood "front face," Past Commander and Grand Master Noble D. Larner, "approaching the East," said to Eminent Commander Thorp, who stood on the neatly draped platform: "Without further detention, it becomes my duty, on the part of the Executive Committee, to say that they have in charge many weary pilgrims travelling from afar, who have been induced to stop at our tents and partake of what we have to give them. It now becomes my pleasant duty to turn them over to your protecting care." Eminent Commander Thorp then addressed them as follows:

It affords me great pleasure to extend to you and the gallant Sir Knights who accompany you a cordial and fraternal welcome, in the name and on behalf of De Molay Mounted Commandery, No. 4. Words seem totally inadequate to express our gratification in thus being honored by your presence, not only on account of the dignity of the high offices which you hold respectively, but also on account of your personal worth as true types of that knightly chivalry which is at once the very foundation and bulwark of our noble Order. Representing, as you do, among your number the varied callings which tend to the promotion and encouragement of private enterprise, industry and progress in two of our sister States, component parts of this great and glorious Republic, we feel proud of the honor of being able to take you by the hand and to greet you in this the Capital of the Nation, as true and worthy Sir Knights. You are now engaged upon a pilgrimage, not such as engaged our illustrious predecessors in past ages, the defense of the Christian religion and the protection of helpless widows and orphans, but to exchange those friendly greetings to which we, as Knights Templars, feel ourselves doubly pledged. Although you are far away from your native soil, the distance only tends to bind our hearts in closer unison, and we trust that our efforts to make you feel at home in our midst will be successful. To the ladies who accompany you, and the ladies of our own jurisdiction, we desire especially to extend our hospitality, and we give them the assurance that, although under ordinary circumstances they have what appear good ground for complaint on account of being excluded from our asylum, on this occasion, at least, we will make an exception to our rules, and admit them to all the privileges accorded to their fathers, husbands and brothers, as Knights Templars. To the Commanderies of this jurisdiction, who have so nobly responded to our invitation to be present, we desire to express our hearty thanks, Eminent Commanders and Sir Knights. Even had I the ability, I would not wish to encroach upon your time by indulging in any extended remarks. I desire only to renew my assurances of the pride with which we hail this auspicious occasion, and to express the hope that you will not measure delight by the very modest arrangements we have made for your comfort and pleasure, but that you will accept our efforts as an earnest of what we might have done had we been possessed of larger experience in such matters. Now, Sir Knights, ladies and gentlemen, we extend to you, one and all, a hearty welcome.

Eminent Commander Rhodes, of St. John's Commandery, in responding, said:

It affords me great pleasure to acknowledge your words of welcome, and in behalf of St. John's Commandery I return my sincere thanks. Their hearts are full, more than full, with gratitude. They were weary pilgrims travelling from afar, but they have not found the rough paths their fathers did, but those filled with pleasure. No matter where they went, the memory of this event would ever remain fresh in their hearts.

Eminent Commander Walbridge, of De Molay, said:

In behalf of De Molay we thank you for this reception, and are deeply grateful for the kind treatment that we have received. We thank you for the courtesy and hospitality that we have been shown on this, our second pilgrimage through this city. We are glad to be received in the asylum of a Commandery of the same name as ourselves, representing the loved Jacques De Molay, the man that lived upright under all oppression and died at the stake for principle.

Rev. W. S. Studley, Past Prelate of De Molay, of Boston, stepped forward and said that he was glad to come to Washington and march under the banners of De Molay and partake of their hospitality. If there was anything that they could do in return, they would do it. This ended the speech-making. The two visiting bands occupied the platform, and for a short time alternately discoursed excellent promenade music. The floor was then yielded to the dancers, and the devotees of Terpsichore enjoyed the pleasure to their hearts' content. It was noticeable that there was very little pretension to rich dressing. The affair was a social event, where Templars and their wives might become better acquainted, pass an enjoyable evening, and pay less attention to Fashion's demands. There was no banquet, but an abundance of refreshments were provided, excellent in quality. It was after midnight before the reception broke and the dancing terminated.

Bright and early on Saturday morning the visiting Sir Knights were astir, and many an old resident of Washington was deluged with queries as to the historical and other facts regarding the National Capital and its peculiarities. By nine o'clock many of the Massachusetts men had become as familiar with the points of interest in and about the city as the oldest inhabitant, and the entire party was eager to participate in the general inspection of the city planned for by the Washington Sir Knights. Soon after nine o'clock carriages were drawn up before Willard's, and the visitors were driven to the White House, to call upon the President. The reception was held in the east room, Past Eminent Commander Noble D. Larner presenting the company to President Garfield. The usual hand-shaking followed, and then, after a very democratic inspection of the White House, the company was driven to the new building of the printing and engraving department. The Rhode Island Senators paid their constituents the compliment of attending the reception at the White House, and Senators Burnside and Anthony greeted each visitor from "Little Rhody," after the presidential hand-shaking. The operations of the printing and engraving departments having been viewed, the Capitol and the Soldiers' Home were visited, and then the Sir Knights and their ladies were driven to a noted German resort, the Schutzen Garden, where a German lunch found very general approval. The return to the hotel was made so as to include a view of the Farragut statue and many public improvements; and, after dinner, conveyances were taken for the wharf, where the party embarked on a steamer for Mt. Vernon. Words fail to convey any idea of the beauty of the scenery and the general pleasure of the excursion. The day was as perfect as that of the poet's ideal June, and the company gave itself over to its enjoyment. The points of interest at Mt. Vernon were duly visited, and the proper things duly said. Soon after arriving the party proceeded to the tomb, and stood uncovered while the American

Brass Band played a dirge. The Commanderies then broke up into squads, and, accompanied by their ladies, scattered over the grounds, visiting the house and inspecting its various rooms. The company remained at Mt. Vernon until near seven o'clock, and then returned to the steamer. Having an abundance of time, a ride was taken almost to Glymont, when the boat "put about" and headed for Washington, where she arrived at nine o'clock. Words are inadequate to describe the pleasure given the visiting Sir Knights during this long day of unremitting attention from the Washington Fraters; not an effort was omitted which could add to the entertainment of the visitors, and friendships were made during its happy hours which will be life long.

Sunday proved an equally enjoyable day, for while many of the Sir Knights followed the customs of New England in attending church, either at the morning or evening service, there were so many kind offers made by the Washington Fraters in the way of social attentions, that the day was variously employed, as individual taste dictated. The morning service at the Metropolitan Church was conducted by Rev. Sir Knight W. S. Studley, D. D., who selected as the text of his discourse, I Corinthians, iv, 5:

> Therefore judge nothing before the time, until the Lord come, who both will bring to light the hidden things of darkness, and will make manifest the counsels of the hearts; and then shall every man have praise of God.

The preacher considered the subject of untimely judgments, and spoke in a way to hold the interest of his hearers to the end, the discourse being listened to by a very large congregation, including a numerous delegation of Sir Knights and their ladies, which would undoubtedly have been more numerous had it not been for the social courtesies extended by the members of the Washington Commanderies. During the afternoon and evening the numerous beautiful drives about Washington were fairly alive with public and private conveyances, filled with the visitors and their entertainers; Arlington Heights, Mt. Pleasant and the Soldiers' Home being the principal points of interest visited. The Washington Sir Knights spared no exertions in their efforts to make the day a pleasant one for their visitors, and the New Englanders fully appreciated the courtesies extended.

IN FREDERICKSBURG.

A GENUINE SOUTHERN WELCOME.—THE PARADE AND ITS CHARACTERISTICS.—THE LADIES VIE WITH THE SIR KNIGHTS IN THE HOSPITALITIES EXTENDED.

THE Sir Knights fell into line shortly before nine o'clock on Monday, May 23, to march to the railroad station, to embark once more upon their pilgrimage, many of the members of the Washington Commands acting as an informal escort and tarrying at the train-house to give a final cheer for Massachusetts and Rhode Island, as the visitors took their departure for Fredericksburg. At about half-past eleven the train arrived at the Fredericksburg station, and the visiting Sir Knights disembarked in the midst of the assembled population of the district for miles around. It was evidently a gala day for all the inhabitants, and joy and satisfaction beamed upon all faces, from the Sir Knights in the lines of the Fredericksburg Commandery, No. 1, drawn up to receive the visitors there, to those of the motley crowd which is seen nowhere but in a Southern town. The ladies were quickly cared for by the Special Committee of the Fredericksburg Command, the private equipages of the town being placed at their disposal, and in these conveyances they were driven to the residence of Eminent Commander Chew, pleasantly situated on one of the main thoroughfares. The line was formed after the usual ceremonies of the reception, and the procession moved through the greater portion of the town in the midst of a blinding dust and almost insupportable heat. The enthusiasm of the improvised body guard which attended the Sir Knights throughout this parade can be but faintly realized by those unacquainted with the peculiarities of the colored people of this section, but it was evident that the heart of the townspeople was in the reception and that the welcome was all that it appeared to be. There was hardly a residence or place of business that was not decorated in some way in honor of the visit, and the word "Welcome" and other appropriate expressions were seen on every hand. The doorways and windows were filled with happy faces, and on every hand was to be seen evidence of an effort to make the visitors feel that their visit had been pleasantly anticipated by all the inhabitants. On arriving at Eminent Commander Chew's residence, the visiting Sir Knights began to realize the warmth of Southern hospitality. The large garden in the rear of the house was spread with tables loaded down with the choicest viands, and the home of the Eminent Commander of the Fredericksburg Sir Knights was thrown open for the entertainment of the guests. The visitors marched into the garden, and when they had been formed in line, Judge J. T. Goolrick, of Fredericksburg, addressed them as follows:

I would not, if I could, pander to any desire for a display of wordy pyrotechnics. I would not, if I could, air my vocabulary with glittering but cobwebbed generalities on this occasion and in this presence, in order to give expression to the great pleasure and high appreciation that we are sensible of by your coming among us, or to emphasize the warmth of our welcome — rather in English unadorned, homely but honest old Anglo-Saxon, I would more faithfully and truthfully represent the sentiments of my people, and respond more cordially to the impulses of my own nature, by saying unto you, simply yet sincerely, we are glad to meet you — glad that you have allowed us the high privilege of giving expression to our sentiments of you — glad that we who live in different sections of a common country have the opportunity of mingling and commingling together, whereby we may know each other better and love each other more. We think that it is right and proper that your first rest should be here on your present pilgrimage to our capital city — a pilgrimage from the land of Lexington to the land of Yorktown — the very Alpha and the very Omega of those struggles that commenced for and culminated in cementing together the Continental States in a free and great republic — a pilgrimage from where Warren bared his breast to the storm of battle and fighting fell, to where Washington struck, with his spotless and stainless sword, from the too tenacious embrace of the then crouching Lion thirteen stars that have attracted to their orbit the grandest constellation that has ever existed in the tide of time. I say in this pilgrimage from the section of our country thus represented to our own, we conceived it right that your first rest should be here — for this spot, be it said, is sacred, hallowed and consecrated not only to the hearts of all the patriotic people of this great land of ours, but it is eminently and pre-eminently so to the great Masonic heart; for here he who was first in war and first in peace first saw Masonic light; here he first trod the tessellated floor, and this is the *alma mater* of Masonry to the warrior-statesman Washington, and his gallant lieutenant, Mercer, and thinking you would gather fresh inspiration as Masons and as citizens, we bade you come to us — dwell even, but for a too short moment in our own tents — and in the name of that obligation which links us together around a common altar, the very granite foundation and keystone of all the temples, that Masonry that was borne far down the corridors of time, that has ever moved majestically and noiselessly onward and upward, having for its clarion cry and shibboleth, "The brotherhood of man," and of that knighthood that received its new birth and another baptism as the cry from hoary England to the banks of the sacred Jordan rose on the air, "Onward to the Sepulchre of Holy Jesus," and legions bearing aloft banners with its red cross and its "*In Hoc Signo Vinces*," moved towards the coveted tomb. In the name of our own great republic, that has been welded together anew by the martyrdom and the blood-treasure of the best of her sons, which bids us be united, though politicians and partisans would drive and keep asunder those whom God himself has decreed shall live together; in the name of a people

who to-day loyally and lovingly march in one unbroken
column under the shadow of the star-spangled banner,
to the moving music of a restored and a reinforced
Union; in the name of our own battle-scarred town,
which we desire shall not meet the expectations or fulfil
the condemnation of that statesman who wrote of it, "It
is finished," until, at least, yon monument shall be completed to mark the spot where sleeps the mother of
him who was first in the hearts of his countrymen, and
until Masonry shall fulfil its high and holy trust of
rearing to the memory of her son — our great exemplar
— a temple which shall at once testify to the world the
character and the life of him who by his practice and
his precepts illustrated and illuminated the teachings,
tenets and principles of our beloved Order, and shall
be as well a very Mecca of Masonry to which we
shall pay the tribute of our high honor, and to which
the Masonic world shall make pilgrimages — and in
the name of this Commandery in whose behalf I speak,
Sir Knights from Massachusetts and from Rhode
Island, I welcome you — not only as Masons, bearing
with us the burdens of a common brotherhood, but as
citizens as well, for around the history of your States
and mine sacred and solemn memories cling and
cluster — memories which ever bear us backward
and bid us look forward. Then welcome — thrice
welcome — to our hearts and to our homes.

Sir Knight Rev. W. S. Studley, of Boston, was
then introduced, and responded most pleasantly
on behalf of the visiting Knights. Referring to
the generous entertainment which had been shown
them in Washington, he said that the evidences of

bounteous hospitality seemed to increase as they went on their pilgrimage, and from the outlay before him he wanted a single line for an epitaph, which was written over many another good fellow's grave, "Killed at Fredericksburg."

Three cheers were then given reciprocally by the different Commanderies, and the Knights fell to the discussion of the bounteous spread beneath the cool shade of the lawn trees. After ample justice had been done to the inner man, an hour or more was allowed for the interchange of social courtesies, an informal reception being held by the Fredericksburg ladies in the cool parlors of Commander Chew's residence. The types of Southern beauty and the refinement and culture of Southern society circles was fully appreciated by the visitors at this reception, and the all too brief stay proved a very pleasant occasion for all the participants. Soon after three o'clock the line of march was again formed, and the visitors escorted to the waiting train, and, after again embarking, the Northern Sir Knights moved onward toward Richmond, followed by the cheers of their entertainers and the assembled citizens, and honored by the waving of handkerchiefs and bright smiles of many of the Fredericksburg ladies, who had driven to the station to give a parting token of their hospitality.

AT RICHMOND.

THE FORMAL RECEPTION.—THE ENTIRE CITY JOINS IN THE WELCOME.—THE ENTRANCE AMID BOOMING CANNON AND CHEERS.—THE VISITORS FEASTED AND FETED FOR FOUR DAYS.

THE run to Richmond afforded the visitors an opportunity to rest from the fatigues of the Fredericksburg march, and, as the train neared the Mecca of their pilgrimage, the Northern Sir Knights prepared themselves for the welcome which they knew full well awaited them. The train arrived at Franklin Street, in the suburbs of the city, at about six o'clock, and the visitors landed upon the "sacred soil" amid the shouts of the immense multitude and the booming of the Howitzer's guns, which were stationed on Broad Street, near the Richmond College; the line was formed opposite the northern end of Monroe Park, and at six o'clock the Providence Commandery in the right of the line reached the stand, which was already occupied by several of the officials of the Richmond Knights. The visitors formed on the west of the grand stand, the Providence Knights being in the advance, and those of Boston massed in the rear. The Richmond Templars faced their brethren, standing on the eastern side of the stand. Eminent Sir Knight Thomas J. Evans then welcomed the visitors as follows:

Sir Knights of Boston and Providence — At the western gates of our city we meet you, to greet you and to welcome you and your ladies, and your guests that accompany you.

In tones of thunder our artillery has saluted you; and now, in tones not so loud, but just as emphatic, we say welcome! In the name of this vast crowd here assembled, we bid you welcome! In the name of a still larger number of citizens not able to be here, we say welcome! In the name of these, our citizen soldiers, who have courteously tendered their services to escort you to your quarters, we extend you a soldier's welcome! In the name of these Richmond Knights, with both hands — one to Boston and one to Providence — we give you a knightly welcome to our asylums, to our hearts, and to our homes. Our tongues would be false to the sentiment of hospitality now glowing in our hearts, if they did not say, in all sincerity, welcome! Many of us have been the recipients of generous hospitalities and graceful kindnesses extended to us by you individually, by your Commanderies, by your citizens, and by your State and city officials.

Why shouldn't we be glad to see you? We are not only brothers of the mystic tie, but we are members of one grand republic. We speak the same language. We live under the same Constitution and National laws. We have a common country. We honor in common the illustrious names of Webster and of Clay, of Jefferson and Adams, of Hancock and of Marshall, of Warren, Greene and Washington. Bunker Hill is ours. Yorktown is yours. The past in our history is our joint inheritance and our undivided glory. The present demands and is receiving our earnest and unbroken co-operation. Our hopes for the future are links in that chain of affection which should closely bind us each to the other. God grant that, as the years roll on, we may be even more firmly united.

De Molay, Richmond, St. John's and St. Andrew's Commanderies form a solid square of fraternal feeling that no sectional or sectarian or political assailants can ever penetrate or break. Being able to frame, to pronounce aright our Masonic shibboleth, you have crossed the Potomac, on which you found all quiet, and not a man of you has fallen. We have met you, and you are ours and we are yours. With arms, but without force, you have passed the lines of the Old Dominion. These swords of yours are not hostile weapons, but with ours and with the glittering blades of all true Knights Templars the world over form a canopy of steel dedicated and pledged to the defence of innocent maidens destitute widows, helpless orphans, and the Christian religion.

Pilgrims, we know that you are weary, and we must therefore no longer hinder or impede you on your journey. We will, however, proceed to examine your scrip and replenish your bottle of water. We will then take you to our tent, where, having performed the necessary ablutions, you will sit down and rest and refresh yourselves. To-morrow his Honor the Mayor will offer you the freedom of our city, to go where you please, to say what you please, to do what you please. And so at present, in the name of everybody in Richmond, without regard to age, sex, condition, or creed, we again say welcome!

The welcome address was briefly answered by Commanders Walbridge of the De Molays and Rhodes of the St. John's, and then the line was formed for the parade to the Exchange Hotel, the headquarters of both Commands. Scenes of enthusiasm rapidly succeeded each other during this parade, as the visitors passed through the crowded thoroughfares to their hotel, and on all sides there were displays of decoration suited to the occasion. The route into the city was by Franklin Street. At the corner of Adams the procession turned into Main Street. One of the pleasant incidents on that thoroughfare was the crowning of the banners of De Molay and St. John's Commanderies by Mrs. J. H. Capers and Mrs. J. V. Bidgood. The wreaths were composed of choicest flowers, etc. The procession turned again into Franklin Street, from Main, at the corner of Fifth, passing by Dr. Hoge's Church on that street. At the residence of Eminent Commander Sir Thomas J. Evans, on Franklin Street, a large banner (adorned with triple crosses) across the street marked the points at which the Knights made a brief halt, and the following young misses gracefully distributed among the visitors their favors in the shape of bouquets: Misses Loulie Evans, Lizzie Brock, Virgie Brock, Hattie Tanner, Mary Cameron, Mary Sheppard, Irene Bodeker, Louise Randolph and Lillian Gilliam. At the corner of Sixth Street the line was turned towards Grace Street, down which the procession moved towards the Capitol Square. As that park was entered the Howitzers fired another salute of thirty-eight guns. The Knights and their escort passed under and by the beautiful Masonic emblems and decorations placed on the Grace-street entrance of the Square. As the line passed the Washington Monument many a knightly chapeau was reverently lifted, and the whole line passed in review before Governor Holliday, who stood uncovered in the front porch of the Executive Mansion, the soldiers, officers and Knights saluting as they passed. Upon arriving at the Exchange Hotel, Sir Knight W. O. English welcomed the guests to their Richmond home as follows :

SIR KNIGHT W. O. ENGLISH'S ADDRESS.

Sir Knights of De Molay and St. John's Commanderies, — You have already heard the kind words of welcome from Eminent Commander Sir Thomas J. Evans.

It only remains for me, as you enter this hospitable mansion to partake of some refreshments and to make it the place of your abode during your stay with us, to add a word, and in the name of the Sir Knights of Richmond to extend to you and your ladies a most cordial welcome, and to remind you of those fraternal feelings which have so long existed between the Templars of Boston and Providence and those of Richmond.

You come not as strangers ; you have been here

before. Even had you been strangers, the greeting you have already received would have been an earnest of our welcome. For what means it that an eager Committee of Reception, unable to await your coming, should start several days in advance to meet you in Washington; that another committee should go to-day to meet you at Fredericksburg, where you were all made prisoners of hospitality by the Templars of that noble old town — a town intimately associated with the early days of Washington and his mother, that model of American women?

Upon your arrival here, what is the meaning of the roar of artillery, which echoing back from the seven hills of Richmond resounds your welcome far and wide? What mean these volunteer soldiers who come so gladly to escort you? What the streaming banners waving from our houses? What the thronging citizens crowding you as you wend your way through our streets? Why is it that the very air is redolent with interest but that we all combine to welcome you to the hospitality of our city? This is the greeting I am here to extend you in the name of all. I welcome you, the descendants of Warren, Hancock, Adams and Roger Williams, to the land of Washington, Jefferson and Patrick Henry; I welcome you to the historic associations of our city, of our river, on whose banks the first American colony was planted; I welcome you to the land of Jefferson, who penned that great charter of American freedom, the Declaration of Independence; I welcome you to the scene of the life of Patrick Henry, the forest-born Demosthenes, who here, in this city, in Old St. John's Church, on yonder hill, uttered those memorable words, "Give me liberty or give me death," which, echoed back by patriotic hearts from the plains of Boston, resounded throughout the length and breadth of the land, and at the summons of a common country and a common cause Virginia sent Washington to the plains of Boston to command the armies of the American Revolution. Thus Massachusetts and Virginia, the two oldest Commonwealths, stood side by side in the great struggle for liberty and independence, and Bunker Hill in Massachusetts, and Yorktown in Virginia, were the Alpha and Omega, the beginning and the end of the American Revolution.

In Virgil, the most elegant of the great classic writers, we read that when Æneas, on his way from the East to found the Roman Empire, landed at the City of Carthage, Queen Dido welcomed him and his weary pilgrims to the hospitality of her palace in these words: *Hunc laetum Tyriisque diem Trojâque profectis Esse velis, nostrosque hujus meminisse minores; Adsit laetitiae Bacchus dator, et bona Juno.* "May this be a joyful day both to the Tyrians [Providence] and to those who have set out from Troy [Bostonians]. May Bacchus, the giver of joy, and good Juno be with us." So, my friends, would we now welcome you, —

> "Sirs, you are very welcome to our house;
> It must appear in other ways than words:
> Therefore I scant this breathing courtesy,"

and cordially invite you, weary pilgrims, to rest and refresh yourselves.

In the evening the ladies of Richmond tendered a reception to the ladies of the visiting Sir Knights at the Richmond Theatre, and the affair proved an eminently enjoyable occasion. The parquet was floored over for the dancers, and an excellent orchestra furnished music for the evening. A pleasant feature of the entertainment was the reading of a poem by Rev. Sir Knight W. S. Studley, called "The Yankee Mirror," in which the peculiar characteristics of New Englanders were happily presented in a vein of good-natured satire. At eleven o'clock the curtain was raised upon a beautiful scene, in which tastefully-set tables, filled with sweets and confections of all kinds, were conspicuous. The refreshments were done ample justice to, and soon thereafter the guests began to disperse, while some lingered to take a parting dance to the inspiring strains of the orchestra. The theatre was profusely decorated, the flags being of all nations and every state in the Union, with the additions of the coat-of-arms of the different states, Masonic and Templar banners, streamers, the English red cross, etc.

The visiting Commands were made acquainted with the desires of their hosts, in regard to the entertainments planned for their pleasure, by a well-arranged programme, giving full details of the various parades, excursions, etc., during their stay, and in conformity with this the line was formed at ten o'clock on Tuesday morning, to proceed to the Richmond Theatre, where the formal reception on the part of the State and city authorities was to occur. The clear skies of the preceding day continued, and the march through the leading thoroughfare attracted a large assemblage of lookers-on. When the Commanderies entered the theatre the audience were seated as follows: Bands in rear of the stage, City Council and officers on the west and in front of them; Judges B. R. Wellford, George L. Christian, Joseph Christian and Hon. J. W. Daniel, with Rev. A. W. Weddell and Rev. Dr. J. B. Hawthorne on the east side. To the front were seated Masonic and Templar dignitaries, lady guests, etc. Governor Holliday occupied a seat on the east side of the stage, as did other speakers. The body of the parquet was occupied immediately fronting the stage by De Molay on the east and St. John's on the west. Immediately in the rear, in the order named, were seated Richmond Commandery, No. 2, and St. Andrew's, No. 13. In the centre of the stage was a handsome floral design, with a cross in the centre, the mottoes above and below forming an Anchor of Hope, with the inscriptions "*In Hoc Signo Vinces*," and "*Magna est Veritas et Prevalibit*." Just in front of this and on either side of it were two other exquisite floral adornments, the gift of Mr. John Morton through Sir Knight P. S. Derbyshire to Richmond Commandery, consisting of a beautiful Maltese cross of scarlet geraniums and roses, and a cross and crown. The crown was about two and a half feet in diameter, of white pinks, calla lilies and white rosebuds, and the handsome cross in carnation double geraniums and red roses made a beautiful contrast with it.

After prayer had been offered up by Rev. Sir Knight W. C. Schaeffer, prelate of St. Andrew's Commandery, Eminent Commander Sir Thomas J. Evans introduced his Excellency Governor Holliday, the Providence band playing "Hail to the Chief" as the Governor stepped to the centre of the stage. As the selection concluded he spoke as follows :

GOVERNOR HOLLIDAY'S ADDRESS.

It is well for the sons of the New England Puritan to visit the sons of the Cavalier in their Metropolis ; it is most agreeable for the sons of the Cavalier to give them cordial greeting in the presence of Richmond's manhood, intellect and beauty.

Old things are passing away, and behold! all things are becoming new. The Puritan has put on the armor and the helmet of the Knight over his work-a-day clothes, and the Cavalier has put on work-a-day clothes over the glittering harness of the Knight. The one has found that there are elevating sentiments that can flourish and fill our daily life with beauty and grace amid the whir of the shuttle and the rattle of the wheel ; the other is learning that there is strength and nobility in labor, which can gather the wealth of nature's vast resources, and bring them with gladness to deck the fields of chivalry.

I bid you welcome, Sir Knights ; whilst together we rejoice in this *renaissance*. You will tell us how your fathers earned the name of " Pilgrim " in their longings after liberty and their sufferings in its behalf ; how they have made the rugged country to which they sped to bloom and blossom as the rose ; how population and wealth have converted the wilderness into the homes of a progressive and cultured people; how their progeny have blazed their way in the van of Empire to the Western Sea.

We will tell you how our sires came to seek a home on this site years before the *Mayflower* landed its crew on Plymouth Rock; how sprung from the loins of those "Sword-smiting Battle-Smiths," who girdled the world with their conquests, they by different modes of thought sought the same ends; how they made it the scene where the conflicts of ideas that were to affect the continent were for so many generations fought, and either won or lost; how from their armory have gone some of the knightliest men who have ever wielded sword or pen for human rights.

And, now, here together we will talk in friendliest sort of how the Gage of battle was joined, and in earnest fight we tested our convictions; of how the glories of a thousand fields have gone to swell the fame of our common blood and lineage; of how peace came, and we hoped a jubilee had also come, when all debts of bitterness and animosity should be forgiven, and the incense of the great sacrifice should strengthen and glorify the new *régime*.

For a new *régime* it is. New England has found that labor can be rendered attractive by the adornment of the gentler graces. Virginia has learned that it does no harm to the gentler graces to have them supported by the vigorous thews of Labor.

Out of this union there will spring harmony and substantial growth for both. History tells us of what your country was, and what it is. How every blow of your industrious has told. The future will speak of us; for already does the bosom of the Old Commonwealth seem to have been touched by Prospero's wand, and there is coming from its vast resources promise of imperial wealth.

And now, if there be any animosities surviving, let them be buried in the graves of our great and loved ones on either side. With chivalric generosity, let us do justice to virtue and valor wherever found. Remitting the camp-followers, the shriekers and the demagogues, both North and South, to everlasting oblivion, let the Puritan and the Cavalier, and their offspring, wherever they may live, rise up in the majesty of a united faith and a fast reconciliation, and command the peace: in that peace we will talk over the deeds of our heroes and martyrs, and the renown they have conferred upon our common race and country, and with high and knightly courtesy and love we will carry their effigies in triumphal procession, and place them side by side in the Republic's Pantheon. We bid you, Sir Knights of New England, cordial welcome to Virginia!

At the conclusion of the Governor's address the Boston band played the "Zampa" Overture, and at its conclusion Rev. Sir Knight Studley, of the De Molay Command, was introduced by Eminent Sir Knight L. L. Bass, and replied to the Governor as follows:

REV. SIR KNIGHT STUDLEY'S REPLY.

I have not been so moved, your Excellency, for many a day as by your magnetic words. I know of nothing that has afforded to my mind a brighter outlook for the future than the sentiment expressed by your Governor, that the laborer has put on his armor over his work-a-day garments, and I believe this country of ours is to be redeemed, if redeemed at all, by Labor.

I believe the day is coming when, as Virginia and New England stood shoulder to shoulder in the struggle for independence, they will stand hand in hand and heart to heart. I have just remarked to the Governor that the Virginians are like Shakspeare's lover, declaring over and over again, "I love you! I love you!" for from the time I and my friends entered Virginia soil we have been treated in this cordial way. I want to say this — that you are always welcome to New England. The doors of our homes are always open, our hearts are always open to you, and all that we have is yours.

As Sir Knight Studley took his seat the Boston band struck up "Carry me back to Old Virginny," and after the enthusiasm over this selection had subsided Mayor Carrington, of Richmond, was introduced.

MAYOR CARRINGTON'S ADDRESS.

Addressing the visiting Commanderies, Mayor Carrington said, in allusion to the ladies that accompanied them :

We thank you greatly for bringing to our homes and hearts your prizes from Nature's matchless studio, and rejoice to be honored by the presence of the female escort of your Commanderies. As is the duty of all chivalrous, knightly men, we of Richmond first pay respects to this protecting outer guard — these fair guardian angels — and greet them with unfeigned welcome. How grand the country, how beneficent the laws, how broad the principles of government must be, when in a land so vast as this the men of every clime can meet, and with peaceful current of common pride, without a thorn of discord to mar their harmony, or repulsive law to jar their interests, and be greeted as I now greet you in that treasured name of "Fellow-Americans." He next alluded to the joint efforts of Virginia, Massachusetts and Rhode Island in achieving the independence of this country in the Revolutionary War. Liberty was cradled in Massachusetts, fostered in Rhode Island, and burst into manhood in Virginia. Grand trio they make — Massachusetts, Rhode Island and Virginia! True types of true Knights and true freemen, well may their hands unite and their hearts flow in golden streams of fraternal friendship.

He ridiculed the idea of a bloody chasm as the creation alone of political marplots. It is said to be

"Home where'er the heart is."

If this be so, then Richmond Knights Templars have homes in Providence and Boston, for their hearts have been with you for years in strongest bond of unbroken love. Distance may have interposed a barrier through which the eye cannot gaze into yours to see responsive loving look, but there is a heart — telephone line that links us to you in never-ceasing current of spirit and of prayer — and by the heaven-born sound of faith's electricity we hear you speak back again. From the classic valley of our James, in Richmond, the love-laden air bears freighted wish up to Boston and Providence that peace may dwell, harmony prevail, and prosperity attend you. And we feel that you make responsive wish and do responsive act for us.

OF THE KNIGHTS TEMPLARS. 51

Then, with this long-established heart-bond, shall it take any words to vouch you welcome, when look and hand and act so plainly say it? We greet you gladly, and bid you freely take our store of good, and only feel regret at the limited supply. It is useless to bid you enter to our hearts, for your noble works and good deeds have already taken possession of that fort; but our homes are open to you — our city and all its beauties and its pleasures we turn over to your control, and declare you welcome to them all.

Generalissimo George H. Burnham, of the Grand Commandery of Massachusetts and Rhode Island, being introduced, responded with a few pleasant and extemporary remarks. He said all the receptions had been so thorough and hearty that the informal reception was enough without the "formal reception." They had been gradually killing him with kindness ever since he put foot on Virginia's soil, and if he really died his widow would have to place the cause at the door of Virginia hospitality. Their hearts, he continued, were full, and language would not express the sentiments of gratitude they felt, and they would like to take each of their hosts individually by the hand ; and returning thanks on behalf of the visiting Knights he hoped they would soon journey North and visit their homes. Sir Knight A. R. Courtney, of Richmond Commandery, No. 2, was then introduced, and spoke as follows :

SIR KNIGHT COURTNEY'S ADDRESS.

Sir Knights of De Molay Commandery and the Commandery of St. John's, — As citizens of Massachusetts and Rhode Island you have been formally welcomed to Virginia, "the Mother of States," by our knightly Governor, in words of earnest and fraternal patriotism, which but echo the feelings of the whole people.

You have been hailed as friends by our Mayor in words of poesy and sentiment, which but express the joy that thrills the hearts of our citizens. And now the Templars of Richmond, your fellow-soldiers of the Cross, come to salute and greet you as pilgrim warriors travelling from afar, and as Fraters of an ancient and honored Order Like the hospitallers of St. John of Jerusalem, whose asylum was always open to the defenders of the Cross, the Templars of Richmond have sent out their heralds to hail you to their asylum; and having provided an abundant supply of good bread and pure water, just such as pilgrims need, in their names and by their commission I bid you welcome, a hearty welcome, to our tents and our temples, our homes, our hearts and our hospitalities.

But not alone as valiant and magnanimous Sir Knights, enlisted under the same emblematic banner, and bound by the same high purposes and principles with ourselves, do we welcome you; these considerations were, indeed, enough to arouse our liveliest interest, and to call forth our kindliest attentions. But in you, Sir Knights, we recognize more than these; in you we recognize our old familiar friends — comrades on many a hard-fought field — our hosts of 1858 and 1875, and our honored and thrice-welcomed guests of 1859. We see before us to-day the same banners that welcomed Virginia Templars to Providence and Boston in 1858, and which the next year waved along our own streets in response to the huzzas of our people, who turned out to welcome you without regard to sect or society — the same banner which was welcomed by floral offerings from thousands of Virginia's fair daughters.

We see here to-day the De Molay and St. John's Commanderies, who met us in 1875 on our pilgrimage to Bunker Hill and Concord, with the same grip and word with which we parted in 1858 and 1859. If affected at all by time and circumstances, that grip was more affectionate and the word of welcome tenderer and heartier than before.

Twenty-two long, eventful years have passed away, Sir Knights, since your former pilgrimage to our shores. During this period "Time, the tomb-builder," has been at work in our ranks, and many of our gallant ones who joined in the happy scenes and brilliant entertainments of your reception on that occasion (among them our then Eminent Commander) have gone before us on their final pilgrimage, and are now at rest in "that house not made with hands." But some of our members who met you on that crusade still survive, and they are all here to-day to welcome you; and the mantles of those who have ceased to answer our roll-call have fallen upon the shoulders of other worthy Sir Knights with whom your names are household words, and they are here also to welcome you.

It matters not whether he be a veteran or a raw recruit in our ranks — whether he be of old Richmond Commandery, which was the immediate recipient of your hospitalities, or of her daughter the Commandery of St. Andrew, born since our last pilgrimage — every Richmond Templar recognizes and welcomes you as their guests, and will vie with each other in doing you honor. Neither time nor death nor internal changes have weakened our attachments for you, or effaced from our memory the recollections of "Auld Lang Syne." Sir Knights, the history of Richmond Templarism is dotted with your names and the names of your Commanderies; and its brightest pages are those which record the events of our fraternal inter-visitations. Those pilgrimages constitute epochs in our history ever to be remembered by our children and our children's children to the remotest generation. The scenes of those days are stamped in living and eternal colors on the camera of our hearts, and there too are drawn in letters of gold your words of welcome and good cheer, and your lofty sentiments of Christian fellowship and fraternity; and as each Spring with its ethereal mildness bursts the obdurate crust of Nature, and perfumes the morning air with the redolent buds and blossoms of May, Providence and Boston, "Rocky Point" and "Downer's Landing," ever and anon rise unbidden before the mind's eye of every Richmond Templar, and he goes to and fro in his daily avocation keeping step to the music of 1858 and 1859 and 1875, which is still sounding in his ear, and enjoys over and over again in imagination your prodigal hospitalities.

St. John and De Molay! Honored names in the past! The lustre of their names is undimmed in your knighthood. Peter, on the Mount of Olives, having cut off the right ear of his adversary, has put up the sword, and has left to you and all true Sir Knights to wage a relentless war in behalf of innocence and the Christian religion, by precept and example. The order of St. John of the twelfth century has passed away, but their valor and magnanimity have made its impress on the great heart of the world. James De Molay, the last Grand Master of Templars of the olden time, has been burned at the stake, but from his ashes truth has grown, and spread over many lands. The Crusades and the Order of Knighthood as it existed at that day have also passed away. The pomp and pageant, the exercises and the games, which accompanied them, are only known in song and story. But that the world is better for their having been, no one can deny. The work which was wrought by Knighthood and the Crusades in scotching the wheels of infidelity, and in advancing the Christian faith, eternity alone will reveal. That they should pass away is but to suffer the lot of all earthly things.

> "All flesh is grass, and all its glory fades
> Like the fair flower, dishevelled in the winds;
> Riches have wings, and grandeur is a dream.
> *   *   *   *   *
> The only amaranthine flower on earth
> Is Virtue; the only lasting treasure, Truth."

But, Sir Knights, the presence of these, your fair ladies, who have undertaken to share with you the hardships of your pilgrimage, is another and an unerring proof of your orthodoxy in the knightly spirit that found expression in the lives of those for whom you are named. Woman was the grand central luminary of the system of knightly orders from its commencement to its close. From woman chivalry drew its light and life, and it was her smile that preserved its being;

and she, on the other hand, true to her distinguishing traits — reverence for religion and admiration for the brave — accompanied her true knight over the seas and desert wastes into the very field of battle. It was hers to buckle on his armor for the fight, and to weave the chaplet for his victorious brow. It was hers to while away his leisure hours with song and story, and all the arts of love; and, "when feverish pain wrung the hot drops of anguish from his brow," it was hers to soothe his soul and to cool his burning brain. To think of a Templar on a pilgrimage without his lady, is to think of an odorless rose, a starless night, or a home without love. She is the Templar's crown and joy; but whether *crown* or *cross*, she reigns and rules supreme, and sooner or later every Knight must be her slave.

"Oh, woman, lovely woman, Nature made thee
To temper man; we had been brutes without thee!"

You are greatly honored, Sir Knights, in having this fair convoy to our gates. They have honored both you and us by their presence; and, more than all, they have not only secured for you a heartier welcome, but without them, I cannot say but that you would have almost forfeited your reception. I bid you welcome, then, gallant Sir Knights and fair ladies — all. Thrice welcome to you, our old friends of the past, and, we trust, our fast friends forever.

A voice from heaven has proclaimed, "Peace on earth, and good-will amongst men." Lay aside, then, the helmet and the shield, the sword and lance, and all the implements of warfare, and come into our asylum and enjoy with us the innocent pleasures of that blessed peace.

Rev. Sir Knight Dadman, Prelate of the De Molay Command, was then called upon, and responded as follows :

REV. SIR KNIGHT DADMAN'S ADDRESS.

Dear Brethren and Sir Knights of Richmond,— Early impressions are said to be the most lasting. Twenty-two years ago, when only a child in Masonry, I was invited, one beautiful May-day, to go out to Roxbury, then in the suburbs of Bostons, and greet the Sir Knights of De Molay Commandery on their return from Richmond. I did so, with many others, and felt it was like greeting pilgrims from the Holy Land; and as I listened to their recital of the events of their journey, the princely reception they met with at the hands and hearts of their Fraters of Virginia, I thought the land did indeed "flow with milk and honey." Like Caleb and Joshua of old, they seemed to have plucked the grapes, and came marching home with the rich clusters upon their shoulders.

From that time to the present that pilgrimage has been alluded to in speech and song as the greatest event in the history of our Commandery. To show you that my early impressions are not exaggerated, I will state what some of the old veterans said to me just before starting: "You cannot have such a good time as we had when we went to Richmond," but we were eager to take our chances.

A happier set of fellows you never saw than were the De Molays when we greeted you at the Hub of the old Bay State. We had *longed* for a chance at you on our own soil, and we did the best we could to pay you off. Now we have come, on your invitation, to perpetuate the friendship, and rivet the golden chain of knightly affection, that we may henceforth be "one and inseparable, now and forever."

There is a beautiful appropriateness in the union between Massachusetts and Virginia. We have literally descended from the same stock, partake of the same nature, and share the same hopes. Both colonies were originally established under one charter (1606) — the London company to be called the "First Colony of Virginia," the Plymouth Company to be called the "Second Colony of Virginia." Therefore we are Virginians, and have come to visit our sister, bound by the ties of consanguinity if not by the divine right of kings.

It is true that some people do rub New England once in a while about the the "blue laws," and say that, under them, "mothers were forbidden to kiss their babies on Sunday;" but that cannot be found upon record. They were rather strict, however; and, so far as the records show, there was but little difference in this respect between the two colonies. Even in good old Virginia absence from public worship cost the absentee a fine of a pound of tobacco, and thirty pounds for an absence of thirty days. A minister's salary was to be paid out of the first and best of tobacco and corn, and no crop could be sold until the church dues were paid; and, besides this, he was to have the twentieth calf, pig and kid. He was forbidden to drink to excess, or play at cards, dice, or other unlawful games.

But, dropping this pleasantry, there is another reason for this union. We were united in the grand struggle for national independence. Old Virginia was the first to occupy the soil, and first to move, in the Continental Congress, the resolution of independence, but the

"Second Virginia" was the first to shed her blood in the American Revolution. You gave us for commander the immortal Washington, and we fought side by side until the final blow of victory was struck at your own Yorktown. Bunker Hill and Yorktown! Washington and Warren!—and these two immortal patriots were distinguished Masons—why shouldn't we love each other?

More than that: the mystic tie of a fraternity founded upon the Christian religion and the practice of the Christian virtues, makes this union beautifully appropriate. It knows no north, no south, no east, no west. It is as broad as the universe. Your own distinguished orator, Patrick Henry, once said, "We are not Virginians; we are Americans." And we say, We are not Bostonians or New Englanders—we are Knights Templars, with hearts as broad as the religion on which our Order is founded, and which points unerringly to a glorious immortality.

We have come from the land of the Adamses, Hancock and Warren; from Concord, Lexington and Bunker Hill, to see the Mother of Presidents—of Washington, Jefferson, Madison and Monroe—to cement a union based upon the fatherhood of God and the brotherhood of man.

Generalissimo George H. Burnham, on behalf of St. John's Commandery, here presented, with appropriate speech, to Eminent Commanders William T. Allen and Thomas J. Evans, of Richmond Commandery, No. 2, and St. Andrew's Commandery, respectively, handsome jewelled badges of St. John's Commandery. Sir Knight Rev. A.

W. Weddell then presented to De Molay and St. John's Commanderies, on behalf of the two Richmond Commanderies, two very handsome swords, which were accepted, on behalf of the two Commands, by their commanders, in brief but eloquent words of acknowledgment. The sword presented to the De Molay Commandery is of elegant design, the hilt being fashioned out of a gold statuette of a Knight in full armor, six inches in height, the right hand resting upon an unsheathed burnished blade, while the blade of the knightly weapon is ornamented with designs of Knights at tilt and in various other positions. The cross-bar of the hilt is composed of emblems of the Order, and the whole is a fine specimen of workmanship. On the scabbard is a figure in bas relief of a pilgrim with scrip and staff, "travelling from afar," and bas relief designs of the Order. The inscription reads:

>Presented by
>Richmond Commandery, No. 2, and Commandery of
>St Andrew's, No. 13,
>of Richmond, Va.,
>to De Molay Commandery, No. 7,
>of Boston, Mass.,
>May, 1881.

The belt and straps are of scarlet velvet, gold embroidered, and the clasp is ornamented with a bas relief of a troop of mounted Knights with lances at rest. The case of the sword is elegantly finished and lined with blue satin, the whole making an elegant gift, which will be jealously guarded

as a souvenir of the Richmond pilgrimage. Rev.
J. B. Hawthorne then presented a banner in behalf
of the ladies of Richmond to Richmond Commandery, No. 2, which was suitably acknowledged by
Eminent Commander William T. Allen, and with
this ceremony the exercises of the morning were
brought to a close.

After the conclusion of the exercises the line
was re-formed, and a tour of inspection of the city's
attractions made. The visits paid to the tobacco
factories proved highly interesting to the guests,
the employés giving not only exhibitions of their
proficiency in handling the raw material, and pro-
ducing the various forms of it in readiness for
market, but adding musical selections of the
quaintest character as they worked. In some of
the factories great pride is taken in the musical
abilities of the men and women employed, and the
songs of the plantation are sung with a peculiar
charm by these native vocalists. While the Sir
Knights were *en route* the streets were filled with
enthusiastic lookers-on, and the visitors were
cheered on all sides. When the Commanderies
were returning from Gamble's Hill Park they were
halted at St. Alban's Hall, Main Street, where an
inspection of that building disclosed the fact that
the Richmond Knights, "with provident care and
circumspection," under the leadership of Sir Knight
Thomas J. Evans, of the committee, had provided
an abundant collation for the delectation of the
inner man of any thirsty and hungry brother

Knight. The provender, liquid and solid, was afterwards enjoyed by the visiting Sir Knights, the Richmond brethren and invited guests. It was the occasion of much pleasant hilarity, as well as a substantial bracer to those who had done a good deal of marching. The Ladies' Committee were meanwhile attending to their duties, and their particular guests were enjoying the beautiful drives in and about the city, the day being thus filled with pleasures for all the Northern guests.

In the evening the Mozart Association, an amateur musical organization, gave an entertainment at its hall in honor of the guests of the Richmond Commands, the attraction being a performance of Julius Eichberg's opera of "The Doctor of Alcantara," with the following cast:

DOCTOR PARACELSUS	Mr. PIERRE BERNARD.
SENOR BALTHAZAR	Mr. SAML. WAGGONER.
CARLOS, his Son	Mr. E. W. HOFF.
PEREZ, Porter	Mr. MONTE WALKER.
SANCHO, Porter	Mr. SAML. WAGGONER.
DON POMPOSO, Alguazil . . .	Mr. H. T. CARDOZA.
DONNA LUCREZIA, Wife of Dr. Paracelsus,	. Miss ISA SMITH.
ISABELLA, her Daughter	Miss MAY THOMAS.
INEZ, her Maid . .	Mad. CAROLINE RICHINGS BERNARD.

The entertainment was a highly enjoyable one, and closed a very happy day for all the Northern visitors.

The events of Wednesday, May 25, will be long and pleasantly remembered by all who joined in the Richmond pilgrimage. The Richmond Commanderies took the members of the De Molay and

St. John's Commanderies, and their ladies, under escort early in the morning, and marched to the river wharf, where a large excursion steamer, brought from Norfolk for the occasion, was in waiting, and the party, with the ladies of the Richmond Knights, in all about four hundred, steamed down the river for a day's sail. On the way down the James to Dutch Gap the events of the war in this vicinity were freely discussed, and much unwritten history of the Richmond siege was narrated by its participants on both sides of the lines. Nearly all the prominent points of interest were seen to have lost all traces of their occupancy during the war; the shores being newly wooded, and the wharves along the river bank, used during the war, having tumbled to pieces and disappeared. Passing through the Gap the sail was continued down to a fleet of monitors, at anchor off City Point, where, through the courtesy of Captain Johnson, the company boarded the *Catskill*, and inspected it throughout. Before leaving the boat "Wally" Reeves conceived the idea of giving the ladies a dance on the fine deck, and a waltz, played by the Providence Band, started the company to tripping the light fantastic very generally. The sail was then continued to Westover, a plantation about sixty miles from Richmond, where a landing was made. The plantation has figured in history for nearly two centuries, and the present manor-house dates back nearly a century and a half. A genuine southern welcome was given here by the ladies of the manor, and an opportunity to see plantation life as it was before the war was afforded the company. The knowledge that there was some "white water" to be had here caused a stampede to the rear porch, where a stately house servant supplied the visitors with water such as had not gladdened their sight for many days. After an hour on the plantation, during which the bands gave a concert on the lawn, and Sir Knight H. C. Barnaby entertained the company with songs and sketches, the party returned to Richmond, the only notable event of the trip being a mock slave auction, in which a picaninny was knocked down to the highest bidder, the price being deposited in a cotton glove, and tied round the little darky's neck as a present from the company. The long but delightful sail afforded opportunities for extended interchange of opinion between the visitors and hosts, which were fully utilized, and a more congenial and unanimous party than that which came back to the city is seldom seen.

The closing events of the Richmond visit occurred on the following day, Thursday, May 26, and it seemed as if a special edict had gone forth from Old Prob., that clear skies and cool breezes should prevail throughout the "Richmond days," for another perfect day was granted for the great parade arranged for. Early in the morning a special order was quietly issued to the De Molays, of Boston, the line was formed without undue commotion, and the Sir Knights marched to Capitol

Square, and decorated the statue of Gen. Stonewall Jackson with flowers. On the march a passing salute was paid Governor Holliday, as the Commandery marched through his grounds, and, after the scene at the Jackson statue, the Command paid a similar tribute at the Washington monument, and then saluted the statue of Washington, in the vestibule of the Capitol, as they marched through the building. During the morning, while the Sir Knights were on the parade, the ladies of the party went sight-seeing through the city, under their special committee's escort. On the march the Sir Knights made a halt at St. John's Church, built in 1740, and at the old Mason's Hall, the first building erected for strictly Masonic purposes in America. Other interesting points were viewed on the march, and the residents along the route decorated their houses, and paid the visiting Commands many compliments as they passed. Miss Van Lew, who held the office of postmistress of Richmond, by President Grant's appointment, decorated her house with portraits of Andrew, Sumner and Grant, in honor of the visit of the Boston Sir Knights, and entertained those who called upon her with many interesting reminiscences of her war experiences. The day being Decoration Day, Hall's Band went to Holyhood Cemetery, and entertained the thousands of visitors there in the afternoon with a concert, while the Providence Band gave a public concert on Main Street in the evening. The series of entertainments planned for the visiting pilgrims closed with a banquet at the Richmond Theatre in the evening, and the end was quite in keeping with all that had preceded. The visiting Commands were taken under escort by the Richmond Sir Knights a little after nine o'clock, and the march to the theatre was an inspiriting event. The streets were one mass of humanity, and on all sides there were displays of fireworks of great beauty, while cheers rent the air as the column of Sir Knights moved onward. On entering the theatre a scene of rare beauty presented itself, the tables for three hundred and fifty guests being set with excellent taste, and, with the gay decorations, the balconies filled with ladies, and the glitter of the brilliant gas lights above and about, an effect of fairy land was almost realized. After the benediction had been pronounced, the ladies withdrew and the serious business of the evening was begun. The menu, in the form of a Greek cross, contained all the delicacies of the season, with a corresponding array of wines. There were three tables extending the full length of the parquette, and five parallel ones across the stage. At the head of the middle table sat Eminent Commander Thomas J. Evans, of St. Andrew's, No. 13, as presiding genius of the occasion. Many of the home Sir Knights stood ready to see that the visiting Knights were well looked to. The banquet progressed to a conclusion, when Eminent Commander Evans read *seriatim* the following toasts, which were repeated at the

other end of the parquette tables by Sir Knight
A. R. Courtney.

THE TOASTS AND RESPONSES.

The eloquence of the evening was largely of an unreportable character, having the sparkle of the true after-dinner effort, which is so utterly lost in its reproduction upon the printed page. There were, however, some of the responses which should be included in a record like this, and none have a stronger claim than the eloquent words of Rev. Sir Knight Dadmun's words in recognition of the toast in honor of "Woman."

TOAST TO WOMAN.

Rev. Sir J. W. Dadmun, in responding to the fifth toast, said :

"Woman," the last, the best, the most beautiful of all the works of God. An intelligent, honest, loving woman is a priceless jewel ; worth more than the most costly diamonds ever possessed or worn by king, queen, or any other potentate. She is an ornament to society, a beacon light to lighten the pathway of all who associate with her. You can trust her with your character and reputation and with untold wealth, and she will never betray you. Her presence makes Nature look more beautiful — the flowers have a richer hue, and their fragrance is more delicious.

Look at that noble, honorable, high-minded young man, as he takes his evening walk with the pure, gentle, loving young lady, whom he has chosen for the companion of his life ; or when he takes a drive along the meadows, over the mountains and through the valleys; or when he takes a sail on the river, or over the lakes and ocean. Did Nature ever before look so beautiful? And what is the cause of this transformation? It is the charms and virtues of a pure, noble-minded woman.

I do not wonder that all the Sir Knights who could do so brought their wives or daughters with them. The sunny South, in this beautiful spring-time, with all her majestic rivers, fragrant flowers, singing birds, rippling brooks, and genial, generous, loving households, will appear much brighter and more beautiful. Our Order makes it our solemn duty to aid "innocent virgins, distressed widows, and helpless orphans." In one State alone (Indiana) our Fraternity has distributed among the widows and orphans of deceased Masons $2,000,000.

In our own Masonic Temple there are two beautiful paintings upon the walls. Both are full-sized female figures. One represents the genius of Freemasonry, and is placed in the centre of the ceiling of Corinthian Hall. In the back-ground is the starry-decked heavens, and in the centre is a full-sized female flying through the air, accompanied by two beautiful cherubs; in her right hand she holds the square and compass — Masonic emblems — which teach us to harmonize our conduct by the principles of morality and virtue; in her left she holds the plumb, which admonishes us to make our passions and prejudices coincide with the line of our duty. The other female figure, which is painted upon the north side of the hall, represents secrecy. The right hand is placed upon the left breast, the lips are closed and compressed with the forefinger of the left hand, teaching the brethren not to divulge to the uninitiated the secrets of our Order.

Now why should we select the figure of a woman to represent secrecy? We answer, because a true woman is the embodiment of beauty and virtue, and *can* keep a secret. Then, you may say, why not admit her as a member? First, the rules of the Order will not admit of it. Freemasonry was originally a society of builders — operative masons — but within the last three centuries it has become more of a social and charitable society, and yet adhering to the fundamental rules of its organization. Secondly, if women were admitted it would give cause for scandal. Scandal-mongers, tattlers and brawlers would gloat over the fact that women were associated with men in a *secret* society, however unreasonable it might appear to us. There is no institution that respects and honors woman more than does Freemasonry.

> "Not she with trait'rous kiss her Master stung,
> Not she denied Him with unfaithful tongue;
> She, when apostles fled, could danger brave,
> Last at His cross, and earliest at His grave."

The response by Sir Knight William B. Isaacs, of the Richmond Commandery, to the toast in honor of the several Commanderies, is also worthy of a place in these records, its words of eloquence arousing enthusiasm on all sides during their delivery.

"THE COMMANDERIES."

In response to this toast Sir Knight William B. Isaacs said:

In a body like this, Eminent Sir, there is generally no necessity for an apology; but it is no less due to you than to myself that it should be known that my mind has for several weeks been full, and for the past several days my mind, my hands, my arms and my heart have been too full for any personal consideration or preparation. The sentiment that has just been drank opens a wide field for comment, and under any and all circumstances should have been entrusted to a mind of more vigor, versatility and comprehension than I claim to possess. De Molay, St. John's, Richmond, St. Andrew, a solid square, cemented by true knightly love, the strongest and purest attributes of the human heart. There is only one solid square under the canopy of heaven of equal strength, solidity, and endurance — that is, "Mother, wife, daughter, sister." This is, Eminent Sir, a remarkable country of ours. Even while looked at through the reflective light of the "Yankee mirror," while the President of the United States does not preside over the same extent of territory, nor rule the destinies of as many people as her Majesty the Queen of England, yet I verily believe he can find within his dominion as great a variety of climate, as great a variety of products, and as heterogeneous mass of people. The trees which are not indigenous to the other, if of any value, are cultivated as an exotic in the other. Why, sir, the banyan tree is indigenous to a portion of her Majesty's dominion, and it has been successfully cultivated as an exotic in this. In the year of 1858 a small band of pilgrims planted its seed in the soil of the States of Rhode Island and Massachusetts, and it at once sprang into active, young and vigorous life. Its boughs were planted in the soil of the Old Dominion in 1859, and, like its parent plant, was vigorous from its youth. It is true, alas, too true, that its spread for a few years was stayed, but, watered by our knightly tears, its life was preserved. In the year of 1875 another band of pilgrims restored its vitality, and now, in 1881, its tendrils are dropped in our soil, throwing its cooling, genial shade, and spreading its beneficent influences over the vast extent of this country, and in its life-giving bowers of love all who are worthy may recline in safety, and without fear of the assaults of section or sectarian, for they can never penetrate or break while protected and defended by the knightly swords of De Molay, St. John's, Richmond and St. Andrew, forming this solid square of fraternal love and affection in which sectionalism or sectarians can never live. .

THE TOASTS AND RESPONSES.

The full list of toasts, and the speakers assigned to respond, is as follows :

1. *Our Guests:* The Junior Wardens of the South call the Worshipfuls from the East from labor to refreshment. Welcome, Zerubbabels, all. Responded to by Rev. Sir Knight J. W. Dadmun.

2. *The Grand Encampment of the United States:* The circle which touches every point in Masonry. Responded to by Sir Knight George H. Burnham, Gene ralissimo of the Grand Encampment of Massachusetts and Rhode Island.

3. *St. John the Almoner:* The patron Saint of Masonry. His name is engraven on our hearts. Responded to by Sir S. B. Swan, of Providence.

4. *Freemasonry:* Hoary with age. Her ancient landmarks have been faithfully transmitted. May her charities ever be as unbounded as the wants of humanity. Responded to by Judge B. R. Wellford, Jr.

5. *Woman:* Mother, daughter, sister, wife. Without her, man would be an Odd fellow and not a Mason. Responded to by Rev. Sir J. W. Dadmun, of Boston, and Sir Knight Parker, of Columbia Commandery, Washington, D. C.

6. *De Molay, Richmond, St. John's, and St. Andrew Commanderies:* They form a solid square of fraternal feeling which no sectional or sectarian assailants can ever penetrate or break. Responded to by Sir W. B. Isaacs and Sir George H. Burnham.

7. *Providence:* Not nearer to Boston than to Richmond. What cheer! Responded to by Sir L. H. Eddy, of Providence (1859).

8. *The Grand Commandery of Virginia:* May she long enjoy the reign o' peace and plenty. Responded to by Sir Knights John F. Regnault and F. A. Reed, of Alexandria.

9. *The Lodge St. Andrew:* The owners of the house from which went the first Red men who ever understood true American liberty. They suited the times to a *Tea!* Responded to by Sir Henry G. Jordan, Senior Warden, of Boston.

10. *Bunker Hill and Yorktown:* The Alpha and Omega of the American Revolution. Responded to by Sir George F. Wright, Captain-General, of Boston, and Judge Joseph Christian.

11. *Washington, Warren, Marshall and Greene:* Names to be remembered and honored as long as Masonry and patriotism are cherished by American freemen. (To be drunk standing.) Responded to by Sir H. P. Hemenway, Generalissimo, of Boston.

12. *Massachusetts and Rhode Island:* The pioneers of civil and religious liberty in America. Responded to by Rev. Sir W. S. Studley, of Boston.

13. *Woman:*
>She rules by right all earthly things,
>Is stronger far than wine or kings;
>Truth alone excels her powers —
>That attribute divine be ours.

Responded to by Sir Pardon Wilbur, of Providence.

FROM THE ABSENT ONES.

The following letters, telegrams and sentiments were read during the evening, by Sir Knight George F. Wright, from absent members:

[From "*Richard III.*"]
Richmond.—" Now civil wounds are stopp'd
>Peace lives again,
>That she may long live here •
>God say — Amen."

SIR GEO. F. WRIGHT, *Captain-General De Molay Commandery.*

Exchange Hotel, Richmond, Virginia.

BOSTON, MASS., May 23, 1881.

My Dear Sir Knight, — As I promised, I sit me down to write a pleasant word to you, though I am sure there is little need, in your case, while your every moment is now replete with happiness from unalloyed enjoyment, in the company of our true and greatly beloved friends, your royal hosts of Richmond. What you are enjoying I can only think of by that anticipation of pleasure I had and cannot partake of. What I did enjoy in Virginia, and particularly in Richmond, in 1859, has not faded from nor palled upon my memory.

I remember the eloquent, whole-souled address of

welcome from Governor Wise, at Aquia Creek, as we first set foot within the borders of Virginia, with courtly grace, in behalf of his friends of Richmond Knights Templars, tendering the homes and hospitalities of all Virginia to us of De Molay — his own executive mansion, with wide open doors for our disposal — presenting a career of regal pleasure for us, the recollection of which still thrills and throbs the hearts of every Sir Knight whose happy portion it was to join in that grand ovation of "unbounded hospitality."

I remember Richmond — our reception at the theatre, the roses showered upon us from its open dome — the great parade in the streets of the city, and the barrels full of aromatic, cooling, comforting liquid, in readiness to quench our thirst, on every street, and at each frequent halt. I remember the ladies — the beautiful ladies — of that lovely city, distributing boquets of fragrant flowers among our Sir Knights all along the route. I remember the armory of the "Richmond Blues," where ice-cooled nectar of "Cliquot" was quaffed from endless streams, from flowing bowls. I remember one occasion, while on a friendly call with Mayor Mayo, I was declared to be a life member of that brave and gallant company; if any yet remain — and God grant there may be many — I send them hearty greeting, and still claim membership. I remember Sir Knight Mayor Mayo. Who that knew him can ever forget his courtly grace, his elegant person and manly form! I delight to remember him, he was "the friend and companion of my youth." How I wish I could call by name every Sir Knight of '59, to recount his deeds of chivalrous courtesy to us. Their loving-kindness will never be forgotten, it is all engraven on our hearts. I remember the banquet; the outpouring of generous sentiment, and the hearty greeting by the unequalled courteous Knights of Richmond. Everything done and said may proudly be remembered, and nothing should ever be forgotten of all that five days happy interchange of courtesies in and by old Virginia.

To recount the whole cannot be told in one short letter; 'tis a tale of joy for every life greeting of ours, and by this time you are tasting and relishing the sweets of a second term of overflowing hospitality from those Knights of 1859, and their worthy heirs and successors.

You know all of 1875 and '76, and I know all of the great value of your services to me — devoted and untiring — so cheerfully given day and night to make the second pilgrimage of the Richmond Knights Templars to Bunker Hill pleasurable and successful. You are now, as Captain-General, associated with your Commander and Generalissimo, entrusted with the honor of De Molay, and I know that you will not let our banner trail, nor the stars of our glory grow dim.

To Eminent Sirs Isaacs, Tanner, Bass, Evans, and to each and every Sir Knight of Richmond and Virginia, I send cordial affectionate greeting.

Of all that remain of '59 let me to them send one shout of joy — one sweet aspiration for heavenly blessing upon each of them.

I have a letter from Eminent Sir Lucien L. Bass, chairman of the Richmond Reception Committee, inquiring as to my being with you, and expressing his desire, and the wish of his command, that I should come with you; to this I made reply, with much regret, that I was obliged to forego the great pleasure of a personal greeting with them on this joyous occasion, and I have from Right

Eminent Sir W. B. Isaacs a reply, official and personal, in terms of affectionate regard, which affect me deeply and sincerely. Pray thank them generously for me, as you so well know how, and give from me a hearty greeting to every Sir Knight of Richmond, for their great attention in thus caring for me.

The struggle between duty here, duty to my own Commandery and to such courteous friends in Richmond was hard for me to bear; and to have lost the pleasure of the lordly greeting you will have and enjoy in Richmond is to lose something of inestimable value that can never again be found.

Sir Geo. L. Clark, my son, sends to you and to the Sir Knights of Richmond love and knightly regard. And as I close I say to you and all of ours :

"O near ones, dear ones,
 You in whose right hands
Our honor calmly rests, our faithful
Hearts all day wide open wait, till
Back from Richmond's royal bands,
 With every joy complete
 You wend your homeward way.

With knightly courtesy,
 I am, your friend,
  JOHN M. CLARK.

BOSTON, MAY 23, 1881.

Dear Sir Knight and Brother,—Will you pause for a moment amid the pop of champagne corks, the rattle of glasses, the smoke of cigars, and the jollity of the banquet, to say a word for one of the home guard, whom cruel circumstances has obliged to remain at home? You remember the Scottish Knight who undertook to carry the embalmed heart of Robert Bruce to Palestine, but in the midst of a fierce engagement hurled the precious relic into the thick of the fight and followed it to his death. I send you my heart, to cast not among enemies but before our friends. Though hard fate has kept me from the fray of good fellowship, my heart is with my noble Fraters of Richmond, St. John's and De Molay. God bless you all! Would I were with you, that my eyes might rest once more upon the manly figures of our Richmond brothers, my hand grasp theirs, and establish once more that electric communication from heart to heart. I have followed your pilgrimage with pride and pleasure, as you have progressed through increasing enjoyments, until you have arrived at that haven of our hopes for years, the home of our Virginia Brothers; have anticipated the joyous greeting and cementing anew, upon Southern soil, of those friendships formed upon Bunker Hill, in old Massachusetts.

I charge you, my dear Sir Knight and Brother, with the almost sacred duty of presenting my dear love to the Templars of Richmond, and especially to those whom it was your pleasure and mine to meet here in Boston. Say to them that the elegant testimonial I received from "Richmond No. 2," couched in such graceful and brotherly language, hangs upon the walls of my home, an object of pride and gratification to me, and all that are near to me, while the "golden cross" will be cherished in my family as an heir-loom and a souvenir of friendship never to be forgotten.

Sir Knights and Brothers gathered together by the "Mother of States," may you march on together in union and love beneath the banner of the Order to earthly prosperity and eternal happiness.

Your friend and Frater,
B. F. GUILD.

BOSTON, MAY 20, 1881.

Dear Sir and Sir Knight, — By the time you read this the De Molay Commandery must have arrived at the Falls of the James, and be enjoying the glorious spring weather, and the historical associations that surround the Capital of "the Old Dominion." The recurrence of the exchange of hospitalities between the Knights Templars of Richmond and the De Molay Commandery of Boston has always been a source of great gratification to those participating in the genial flow of friendship and good cheer that has marked their advent for over twenty-one years past. I well remember about that time ago, seeing the Richmond Commandery march through the streets of Boston in a style of drill and equipment that impressed the public as well as myself with the highest admiration for their knightly bearing. They were a noble specimen of the descendents of the Old Cavaliers. It was directly after their visit, whilst the warmth of admiration was still lingering, that I became a member of the Order, and of De Molay Commandery. Although, unfortunately, public avocations prevented my going with De Molay Commandery on their visit to their Richmond friends shortly afterwards, the exuberance of enthusiasm which, on their return, they manifested for the genial and fascinating welcome they had received, will never pass from my memory.

When the obstacles growing from political disturbances had ceased, how quickly the old love of these two Commanderies embraced the earliest occasion to blaze forth in its full, cheerful and kindly flame. You came to hearts and halls that were full of welcome, sympathy and affection. There was no gap in the old stream of knightly brotherhood; it flowed with the same constant and deep stream which had marked it in the olden days. So may it always flow. We found the Richmond Knights as of yore; their heads were hard, their digestion good, their legs strong, in the weary march, and their bearing showed all that chivalry and warm hearts can yield of grace and courtesy. The dignity and eloquence of their oratory shed a grace on the festivals they participated in, which none of our Boston Commandery are likely soon to forget. It was a rich treat to us; I trust its memories are equally pleasant to them.

Now, my dear Frater, I am again deprived, because of the sessions of our courts, from accompanying the De Molays to Richmond; from seeing that fair city, grown more beautiful, populous and prosperous than she was when I last saw it in 1844; from seeing her *now*, when, with her developed railroads, connections and various industries, she bids fair to become one of the great commercial and industrial centres of the North American continent, and to impress her stamp upon its civilization of the future, as her great statesmen, philosophers and orators have impressed theirs upon the institutions and constitutions of the holy union whose destinies and mission are not unfolded.

I pray you, then, for me, to renew to my old friends of the Richmond Commandery the expressions of my kindest regards; my heart is marching with you, though in body I am absent. I depute you, and from your high rank, and being often tried, I know you are well capable, to drink for me of the "peach and honey," and the "morning mint," in those customary oblations to the grim malaria which, about this time, in the spring,

Richmond doctors recommend. Remember me in all kindness to the Fraters of De Molay, and tell them that occasions like these build for Freemasonry and for Knight Templarism a Temple in the human heart, decorated with the noblest virtues, a monument more striking than lofty pinnacles or fretted domes, a fountain of charity, fraternity and hopefulness, perennial and perpetually flowing for the progress and elevation of the human race.

  Fraternally yours,
  CHAS. LEVI WOODBURY.

BOSTON, MAY 19, 1881.

CHARLES B. LANCASTER, *Past Eminent Commander:*

Dear Sir Knight and Brother, — After leaving you at the station this evening, and seeing you off so gay, my own regret at *not going with you* was so strong I feel impelled to write a few words, "that not being present" I cannot speak; and first let me assure you and our Richmond friends of my *unfeigned regret*, that *nothing* but imperative business at home would have prevented my being with you in Richmond.

As you left to-day such a world of associations came flooding back on my memory, and all so full of delightful recollections. I saw, in memory, the reception of our dear Richmond friends in Boston, in 1858, now twenty-three years since, and again I saw that never to be forgotten reception we had, and I led, at Richmond in 1859 — dear old Brothers Winslow Lewis, John Flint, Charles Robbins, and last, but not least, our dear old General Tyler, that man of perennial youth — and from Richmond; good old Dr. Dove, sainted and beloved, Mayor Joseph Mayo, McMurdo and all that gallant Richmond host — such a galaxy of knightly forms — they all have passed on; but, with what precious memories, and how sweetly garnered in all hearts.

And, now again we are to be received on Virginia's sacred soil, I send you all my heart-felt greetings; let joy be in every heart, and every face shine with gladness; let knightly hospitality warm every heart; let every Sir Knight feel we are one in purpose, and a part of a great nation; let patriotic hearts be stirred to say good things; and may the golden band of knightly love bind all our hearts, to make us true patriots of our now glorified and united republic.

In knighthood's bonds,

WILLIAM PARKMAN.

Subjoined was the following volunteer toast:

Our Country — may its glorious stars and stripes be gallantly defended by every knightly sword, and all hearts, united as one, by the golden bonds of knightly courtesy and hospitality.

BOSTON, MASS., May 25, 1881.

SIR KNIGHT WM. B. ISAACS, *Grand Recorder*:

Please present at the banquet the following from the Grand Master: "Virginia and Massachusetts and Rhode Island; united in Templar Masonry by the laws of mutual confidence and a fraternal love, we march forward on our mission of benevolence and virtue, with a common purpose, a common faith, and an abiding hope of future progress of Templar Masonry throughout the jurisdiction of the United States."

BENJ. DEAN.

BOSTON, MASS., May 24, 1881.
EMINENT COMMANDER F. G. WALBRIDGE, *De Molay Commandery K. T. :*

Congratulations to De Molay and St. John's in your pleasant festivities. Remember us in knightly courtesy and brotherly love to all our Fraters, and especially to Richmond Commandery.

W. H. KENT,
Grand Commander.

PORTSMOUTH, VA., May 26, 1881.
SIR KNIGHT WM. B. ISAACS, *Grand Recorder Knights Templars* :

Indisposition and business keeps me from being being with you to-night, which I regret. Please say for me, though, to our friends : The first permanent settlement of our country was made in Virginia; the first in the northern portion was made in Massachusetts. The Revolution commenced in Massachusetts, and ended in Virginia. George Washington the first President, John Adams the first Vice-President; John Adams the second President, Thomas Jefferson the second Vice-President. The first years of our country were made by Virginia and Massachusetts. We will never yield our interest in the monument at Bunker Hill, but will be ever ready to protect Massachusetts' interests in the monument to be erected at Yorktown.

J. G. BAIN,
Past Grand Commander.

BOSTON, May 22, 1881.

The Sir Knights of the Richmond Commandery— They will stand upon the record of time as the representatives of a principle that, while it gives life and harmony to the nation, it provides for man the beautiful means of domestic and social happiness in society.

A '59 VETERAN.

P. S.— Don't you get tuckered out.

ELISHA G. TUCKER.

The ladies were by no means neglected while the Sir Knights were thus enjoying the pleasures of the festive board, for the committee having their entertainment in hand provided an elegant supper at Pizzini's, near the theatre, which was most thoroughly enjoyed by their guests. These events concluded the entertainments provided for the Northern guests by their Fraters of Virginia, and a more successful series of pleasant reunions could hardly have been devised. The stay of the Massachusetts and Rhode Island Sir Knights was made a continuous ovation, in which not only the members of the Order participated, but every resident of Richmond as well. Go where they would the Northern men found that the Southerners were ever ready to anticipate their wishes; attentions of every kind were showered upon the visitors, who were made to feel that the city had in reality opened its doors for their entertainment and enjoyment. A notable prominence was given all the events of the visit by the Richmond press, and its representatives showed a degree of enterprize and energy in chronicling all the happenings of the several entertainments which could hardly be surpassed by their Northern contemporaries. Many kindly courtesies were extended the *Herald* representative during his stay in the city, for which he desires to thus formally tender thanks. The editorial utterances upon the events of the visit were of great interest, as they reflected a sentiment highly complimentary to the Richmond people, and proved that the welcome given the visiting Sir Knights was a sincere one.

IN BALTIMORE.

The Monumental City gives a Hearty Greeting to the Pilgrims. — An Evening Reception and Banquet by Beauseant Commandery. — A Short but Enjoyable Visit.

ON Friday morning the Massachusetts and Rhode Island Sir Knights were formed in line again, and, under escort of their entertainers, took up the march to the railroad station for their return journey. The route through the city was one continuous succession of ovations, the residents turning out in crowds to pay a parting tribute to the visitors. On arrival at the train the usual courtesies were exchanged between the visiting and resident Commanderies, and the train moved away from the station amid grand demonstrations from the assembled multitudes, which included a large number of ladies of the Richmond Sir Knights, whose attentions had added so much to the pleasures of the visit. At Fredericksburg a large party of the Sir Knights and ladies met the train, and exchanged good wishes with the homeward-bound pilgrims during a short stop, and at Washington a stop was made for dinner, and here, also, a large company of Sir Knights and ladies renewed the pleasant acquaintance of a few days before during the brief stay. The train arrived at Baltimore at four o'clock, without further incident, and, upon disembarking, the Pilgrims found themselves again captured by the friendly Knights of the monumental city. The visitors were met by Beauseant Commandery, the officers of the Grand Commandery of Maryland, and delegations from Maryland, Baltimore, Monumental and Crusade Commanderies. A large number of the Baltimore Sir Knights were assembled upon the platform, and these first gave a welcoming hand to the visiting brothers. The ladies accompanying the party were escorted to coaches provided for them by the committee, and driven to the Carrollton and Barnum's, where quarters were assigned them. The visitors quickly formed in line upon the platform, and thence proceeded to the Charles-street entrance, where Beauseant Commandery was drawn up to receive them, and where the customary honors were duly accorded. The line of march was then taken up, the escort moving in the following order:

Platoon of Police.
Fifth Maryland Regiment Band.
Maryland Grand Encampment — Right Eminent Grand Commander C. B. Kleibacker, Eminent Grand Generalissimo Woodward Abrahams, Eminent Grand Prelate Joseph F. Hinds, Eminent Grand Senior Warden C. C. Isaacs, Eminent Grand Junior Warden Wm. F. Cochran, Eminent Grand Treasurer Charles W. Hatter, Eminent Grand Recorder Charles T. Sisco,

Past Grand Commanders Henry W. Marston, Wm. Tell Adreon, Jacob E. Krebs and F. J. S. Gorgas.

Beauseant Commandery, No. 8 — Thomas J. Shryock, Eminent Commander; Harry A. Barry, Generalissimo; George M. Taylor, Captain-General; John B. Oldershaw, Senior Warden; W. W. Abrahams, Junior Warden; Past Eminent Commanders J. Kos. Parker and Frederick J. Kugler.

Maryland Commandery, No. 1 — Past Eminent Commanders E. J. Oppelt and Charles G. Edwards.

Baltimore Commandery, No. 2 — W. E. Oppelt, Eminent Commander; James S. Gorman, Generalissimo; Thomas McCoubray, Captain-General; Past Commanders H. O. Reese, W. H. Clark and J. A. C. Kahler.

Monumental Commandery, No. 3 — Thos. W. Griffin, Eminent Commander; James Young, Generalissimo; James P. Clark, Captain-General; Past Commanders, J. L. Bump, Charles McDonald, Jr., and Franklin Hopkins.

Crusade Commandery, No. 5 — S. R. Mason, Eminent Commander; Charles W. Webb, Captain-General; Past Commanders, George H. Mason, Joseph E. Tyler and Dr. M. W. Donovan.

In Baltimore, as in Richmond, the welcome extended by the Sir Knights seemed to be fully seconded by the citizens of all classes, for the visitors were cheered and made the object of ovations all along the line of march to their hotels. A reception and banquet were tendered the visitors in the evening at Masonic Temple. The auditorium, where the reception took place, was tastefully decorated with banners and emblems of the Order, and upon the stage was a beautiful display of tropical plants. Over the stage was suspended the velvet and gold banner of Beauseant Commandery, and below, a design with the words: "Welcome, Knights of the Temple." The Reception Committee escorted the visitors from the hotels to the Temple, and at nine o'clock the assembly was called to order by Right Eminent Grand Commander C. B. Kleibacker, who spoke as follows: "Knights of the Temple, we greet you. What we have anticipated for the past few months we realized this afternoon in receiving, and this evening in entertaining you, valiant Soldiers of the Cross from the East. The duty imposed upon me is to introduce you to our Fraters. All I can say is, make yourselves feel and be at home. All of you thoroughly understand the meaning of this term. And if, after our few hours' entertainment, on your way home you will only remember that you met us in Baltimore, we will be more than amply repaid. Boston, we greet and welcome you. Providence is with us, and ever will be. Washington and Richmond entertained you; Beauseant will take care of you on your way to Palestine. And I have now the pleasure of introducing to you his honor Mayor F. C. Latrobe." The mayor, who was greeted with applause, said:

MAYOR LATROBE'S ADDRESS.

Sir Knights, — You have marched a long distance on this your pilgrimage from the North. You have visited the capital of the nation, and paid your respects to the Great Father in Washington. You have proceeded further South, and in the capital of the Old Dominion have been welcomed by the governor of the mother of States. On your homeward journey you have been pleased to halt at Baltimore. I bid you welcome to the Monumental City, and I beg that you will tarry with us awhile, and accept some of our Maryland hospitality. [Applause.] The States of Massachusetts and Rhode Island, from whence you come, are well known for their prosperity, and the people of those States have a well-earned reputation for energy, good citizenship and patriotism. New England was the cradle in which Liberty was rocked in this land; and if we in the South had our Yorktown and Cowpens, it was Massachusetts which gave us Concord, Lexington and Bunker Hill. As every good Mahometan expects, at one time during his life, to visit the shrine of the great prophet at Mecca, so should all good Americans make a pilgrimage to Boston and stand beneath the shadow of the tall column which marks the place where the first great battle for independence was fought. Nor should the pilgrimage end until after a visit to Annapolis, in Maryland, where, in the Senate Chamber of the old State House, General Washington resigned his commission in the army, and sheathed forever his victorious sword. We are especially glad that, ignoring the practice of the Knights Templar of old, who travelled alone and on horseback, you have brought with you some of the fair daughters of New England. They are doubly welcome to our city, and all that courtesy or chivalry suggest to make the welcome a cordial one will, I know, be extended by the

Knights Templar of Baltimore. [Applause.] Coming hither as pilgrims, we hope that you will, during the evening, enter our tents and partake of some refreshments, after your long and weary march. I regret, however, to inform you that the commissary department of the Baltimore Knighthood is somewhat affected by the season of the year in which you have begun your pilgrimage. Usually, it is the terrapin, the oyster and the canvas-back which furnish our daily rations, but now the two former are replaced by a crustacean known as the hard-shell, and the latter as the soft-shell crab. Both, I assure you, are very palatable, and indigenous to the waters of the Chesapeake. Nor will these refreshments consist of bread and meat alone, but after awhile we shall propose that you join with us in pledging the health of those ladies of Boston and Providence, coupling with it those of Baltimore, who are present on this happy occasion, when we bid you, Sir Knights of New England, welcome to Baltimore.

Sir Knight George H. Burnham, of St. John's Commandery, and Grand Generalissimo of the jurisdiction of Massachusetts and Rhode Island, responded on behalf of the St. John's and De Molay Commanderies. He spoke of the general greeting which had been extended to them all along the line, and said they never could forget the handshaking they had received. Since leaving the dear old scenes of home they had been greeted by knight after knight, and ladies too, all with outstretched arms and hands. It was quite a task to go through with such a journey, but the burden had been lightened by the residents of the country through which they had passed. The speaker then referred to the visit being a return one of twenty-two years ago, and spoke of there being Sir Knights now in the Commandery who had made the first trip. "We," said he, "who did not make the visit, were told of the hospitality of Virginia, and this made us anxious to go. We have realized that hospitality." In conclusion, Sir Knight Burnham referred to the fact that he had before visited Baltimore, on the occasion of the triennial conclave, and was much pleased to have an opportunity to renew the pleasant acquaintances made at that time. Mr. Wm. S. Young, President of the Corn and Flour Exchange, was next introduced, and made a happy speech. He said he was not a Mason, and therefore should call this an extraordinary occasion. The reason for his not being a Mason might be because he had been brought up in the country, where a Mason was only known as one who built houses for the people. Practically, therefore, he knew nothing of Masonry. "I do know," he remarked, "and I believe, your institution will, at the last great day, receive the Divine greeting of 'well done,' and can well and truly say, 'Now have I finished the work Thou gavest me to do.'"

Mr. Young proceeded by telling the visitors that if the Sir Knights of Beauseant Commandery did not properly care for them, all they had to do was to put themselves under the protection of the young men of the Corn and Flour Exchange, who would show them all that was to be seen, even if they did belong to an institution whose members "did all the harm they could, consistent with human depravity, to their neighbors."

Sir Knight Thomas J. Shryock closed the addresses of the evening by welcoming the visitors in behalf of Beauseant Commandery, saying that although it might be considered superfluous, after the remarks of Mayor Latrobe, he would still be a recreant to Beauseant Commandery if he did not add a word of welcome from the heart. For love of ladies knights of old did desperate deeds of valor, and although we of modern times cannot splinter a lance in their behalf, we can say, at least, that the respect and esteem of knights of old burns as brightly in our hearts ; and while this welcome may not be as brilliant as those previously accorded you, it is no less hearty. Following the addresses the following musical programme was presented and listened to with pleasure, Sir Harry Sanders being the director, and Mr. W. M. D. R. Muller the accompanist:

TRIO — *Guai! se te sfugg un moto* — *from "Lucretia Borgia,"* . . . . . . Verdi.
MISS AMY ROGERS, MR. HARVEY PASSAPAE and DR. B. M. HOPKINSON.

SOLO, SOPRANO — *O Luce Di Buist Amina*, Donizetti.
MISS AMY ROGERS.

SOLO, BARITONE — *The Creole Lover*, . Dudley Buck.
DR. HOPKINSON.

Solo, Piano — *Fantasie, "Tannhauser,"* . Liszt.
    Mrs. W. M. D. R. Muller.
Solo, Tenor — *Pure is Her Soul, "Mignon,"* Thomas.
    Mr. Harvey Passapae.

A banquet followed in Corinthian Hall, which was decorated with evergreens and plants. There were a number of tables spread, the centre one being in the form of a cross. Plates were laid for seven hundred guests. After the banquet there was a hop, which continued until early in the morning, and the evening's pleasures were heartily enjoyed by all who participated in them, notwithstanding the fatigue incidental to the day's ride and the parade on arriving in the city. A large number of the visiting Sir Knights and their ladies were astir early the next morning, and took a carriage drive in the beautiful suburbs of the city, the line being formed for the march to the station at ten o'clock. Just as the De Molays were leaving their hotel, a magnificent floral facsimile of the triangular medal issued by Maryland Encampment, No. 1, in 1881, making a design nearly three feet long on either side, was sent to the Boston pilgrims by the members of Maryland Encampment, and this was carefully transferred to Boston by the Commandery. The train moved out of the Baltimore depot amid the cheers of the assembled Commanderies, and reached Jersey City on time without further incident, the ride being an intensely fatiguing one, on account of the great heat.

THE NEW YORK RECEPTION.

PALESTINE COMMANDERY OFFERS SHELTER TO THE PILGRIMS. — A LUNCH AT MASONIC HALL. — AN ENTHUSIASTIC GREETING. — THE STREET PARADE. — OFF FOR BOSTON.

THE special train conveying the returning Sir Knights and their ladies reached Jersey City at about four o'clock, a little ahead of schedule time, the prompt movement of the party having been continued throughout their Southern tour. On crossing the ferry, under escort of a committee from the Palestine Commandery of New York City, the Sir Knights of the Command were found drawn up in line ready to extend courtesies to the homeward bound pilgrims. In West Street a procession was formed, and until Canal Street was reached the Boston men marched ahead. After that the New York Commandery, preceded by Arbuckle's 9th Regiment Band, took the lead. The line of march was through Canal Street, Broadway, Fourteenth Street and Sixth Avenue, to the Masonic Temple, at Twenty-third Street, where the Boston Commandery was welcomed by John A. Lefferts, Eminent Commander of the Palestine Commandery. The march was a very fatiguing one, and few formalities were indulged in before the Boston Sir Knights were escorted to the chapel of the temple, where an elegant lunch had been spread. Such hospitality as was here shown is rarely experienced by weary pilgrims, but its attractive features were fully appreciated, and the heartiest sociability was enjoyed by the entertainers and the entertained. After a time an attempt was made at a semi-formal interchange of good wishes, brief speeches being made by Sir Knights George W. Walgrove, Charles J. Bliven, A. Wiennett Peters, Charles A. Atkinson, Edwin Dodd, Peter Forrester, T. Preston and John Scott, of the Grand Commandery; Thomas B. Rand, R. H. Brockway, Edward S. Eunson and John F. Baldwin, of the Palestine Commandery ; and Eminent Commander F. G. Walbridge and the Rev. Sir Knight J. W. Dadmun, of the Boston Commandery. These speeches were mainly of an unreportable character, admirable when listened to, but lacking the characteristics to make them interesting in such a record as this. Rev. Sir Knight Dadmun's response for the Boston Commandery was, however, of a nature eminently suitable to recall the fraternal sentiments which were exchanged by the Sir Knights of the two cities on this occasion. It was as follows :

REV. SIR KNIGHT DADMUN'S SPEECH.

Eminent Commander, — I cannot find language to express to you, and your Command, the gratitude we feel for this magnificent banquet you have so kindly spread before us. We have heard of your fame, not only as wise and accomplished Masons, but as liberal, courteous and gallant Knights Templars. The reception you have given us to-day, on our return from Richmond, goes far beyond our most sanguine expectations, and we assure you, as weary pilgrims travelling from afar, that we are in just the right mood to appreciate this outpouring of your unbounded hospitality.

One of the speakers has just said, "The De Molays have taken Richmond," but I think that Richmond has captured the De Molays; and it was on this wise: Some three months ago we received from the Richmond Sir Knights a challenge to meet them, on Virginia soil, and decide one of the grandest contests that ever engaged the hands and hearts of valiant Templars. We promptly accepted the challenge; and, having the choice of weapons, chose the greatest and most beautiful armor ever worn in mortal combat, which is LOVE. We thought we could wield that keen and penetrating lance as effectually as any body of Templars that ever marched out to battle. Armed and equipped as the law directs, we quietly passed through your city, and were undisturbed until we reached Washington.

The Sir Knights of the Capital, having heard that we were going to invade the South, turned out *en masse*, headed by the Washington De Molays, mounted, and nearly discomfited us before we reached our destination. We recovered, however, and in good order boldly marched into Old Virginia; but when we reached Fredericksburg we found the Knights Templars and all the men, women and children drawn up in battle array, the drums beating, cannons booming, and the grand old flag of the Union waving upon every hill and housetop as far as the eye could see, determined to dispute our progress. For full three hours the strife went on, until we were forced to retreat, or run the risk of having for an epitaph: "Killed (by kindness) at Fredericksburg."

These skirmishes made things lively for our gallant little band, but when we reached the Capital of the Old Dominion, and saw the plumed cavaliers, supported by the artillery and infantry, and fifty thousand citizens, we felt about as small as did that little Spartan band who so heroically defended the pass of Thermopylæ. For four days, amid the waving of banners, the booming of cannon, and the illumination of fireworks, the glorious strife went on. We first made one grand attack all along the lines — a *hand to hand* conflict, give and take — and I am sorry to say that, on *our* part, there was more *taken* than given. After a two days struggle we retired to our quarters and held a council of war. We determined the next day to mass our forces, and make one grand attack on their centre. Early the next morning (it was Decoration Day in Richmond), having procured two beautiful wreaths of flowers, we surprised the whole city, even our Fraters of St. John's Commandery, by moving out in solid columns to Capitol Square, and there depositing one of the wreaths at the foot of the famous English statue of that Christian and hero, Stonewall Jackson; the other floral tribute was laid at the base of Crawford's grand statue of the immortal Washington and his great revolutionary compeers. The effect was irresistable; the centre gave way; strong hearts melted; old veterans wept like children, and were not ashamed of their tears.

They soon recovered, however, from this startling

surprise, reformed their broken ranks, and made one desperate onset, turning our right and left, and completely surrounding us. They then proposed, as terms of peace, an alliance, offensive and defensive, to which we gladly assented; *and we all, then and there, formed a solid square, bound by the golden chains of* LOVE *and* KNIGHTLY CHIVALRY, *which neither sectionalism nor sectarianism can ever penetrate or destroy.*

In a word, Sir Knights, our pilgrimage has been one grand series of ovations. At Richmond, our objective point, his Excellency, the Governor, welcomed us in one of the grandest Union speeches that ever fell from mortal lips. His Honor, the Mayor, followed him with an eloquent address, "keeping step to the music of the Union." Then Sir A. R. Courtney, in behalf of the Templars of Richmond, welcomed us in a ringing speech, full of knightly courtesy and good cheer; and the women, as they looked down upon us from the gorgeously decorated galleries of the theatre — where we were assembled — with their sparkling eyes, glowing cheeks and smiling faces, seemed like angels from heaven on missions of love and good-will to all.

On our return, we received a most cordial and knightly greeting from our Fraters of the Monumental City; and this morning, as we were about to leave Baltimore, the old Maryland Commandery, No. 1, gave us a genuine surprise, by presenting the De Molays with an elaborate floral tribute of exquisite beauty and workmanship. And last, but not least, you have overwhelmed us with this princely reception. Again, in behalf of the officers and members of the De Molay Commandery I sincerely and heartily thank you."

Immediately after the close of the sumptuous banquet given by Palestine Commandery, the following telegrams passed between Richmond and New York:

NEW YORK, May 28, 1881.

SIR WILLIAM B. ISAACS:

From your *Fraters* of the second colony of Virginia. All's well. You have conquered us by the divine attribute of love. We are your willing subjects. Sectionalism was forever buried when our boys placed a wreath on the statue of the Christian and hero, Stonewall Jackson.

J. W. DADMUN.

De Molay Commandery.

The following reply was immediately flashed over the wires:

RICHMOND, May 28, 1881.

REV. J. W. DADMUN, *St. Nicholas Hotel, New York:*

The *Fraters* of the first colony send their loving remembrances to its conquered children. All's well. The act of crowning made the square solid. Neither sectionalism nor sectarianism can ever penetrate the household or break the ties that bind us. Love to all hands.

WILLIAM B. ISAACS.

After this interchange of courtesies the line of march was reformed, and the Boston Sir Knights escorted to the St. Nicholas Hotel, where quarters had been assigned them for the night and the following day. Upon the arrival of the train at Jer sey City a special committee had received the ladies of the visiting Sir Knights, and they were escorted to carriages, and driven immediately to the hotel, where they were entertained at lunch by the ladies of the Sir Knights of the Palestine Commandery. After dining the Boston Sir Knights were the guests of individual members of the Palestine Commandery, and the same courtesies were extended during the morning of the Sunday following. At about four o'clock on Sunday afternoon a large delegation from the Palestine Commandery met the Boston Sir Knights at the St. Nicholas, and without music of any kind, in compliance with the city ordinances, took the returning pilgrims under escort to the Fall River boat, where friendly parting greetings were exchanged, and the Boston Sir Knights turned their ways to the Hub, passing a pleasant night on the Sound, breakfasting on board the boat, and then, by special train for Boston, arriving home at about nine o'clock, and landing at the Old Colony Depot in a flood of sunshine, which made the city look even more attractive than usual to the wandering pilgrims.

THE HOME RECEPTION.

The Boston Commandery Extends a Cordial Greeting. — A Street Parade and Banquet. — The Welcome Speeches and Congratulations. — The De Molays Dismissed.

ON the arrival of the train the Sir Knights of the De Molay Encampment found the Boston Commandery of ten companies drawn up to receive them, and upon forming in line the usual courtesies were exchanged. The roster of the Boston Commandery on this occasion was as follows :

Sir J. Francis Lotts, *Eminent Commander.*
" John L. Stevenson, *Generalissimo.*
" Edwin Wright, *Captain-General.*
" Rev. John P. Bland, *Prelate.*
" Eugene H. Richards, *Senior Warden, in Command of the Lines.*
" James M. Gleason, *Junior Warden.*
" William Sawyer, *Acting Treasurer.*
" Zeph. H. Thomas, *Recorder.*
" Edward Storer, *Acting Standard Bearer.*
" Joshua F. Sampson, *Sword Bearer.*
" William A. Bunton, *Warder.*
" George W. Bunton, *Third Guard.*
" Eugene A. Holton, *Second Guard.*

Sir EDWARD COGGINS, *First Guard.*
" CHARLES F. ATWOOD, *First Assistant Guard.*
" WILLIAM L. LATHROP, *Second Assistant Guara.*
" CHARLES H. BALDWIN, *Third Assistant Guard.*
" JOHN B. RHODES, *Musical Director.*
" ALEX. K. BRYER, *Armorer.*
" BENJAMIN F. NOURSE, *Sentinel.*

CAPTAINS OF COMPANIES.

First Company,	. .	Sir GEORGE E. HALL.
Second "	. .	" WM. H. BURROUGHS.
Third "	. .	" JOHN H. NORTH.
Fourth "	. .	" EDGAR F. HUNT.
Fifth "	. .	" JOHN S. DAMRELL.
Sixth "	. .	" HENRY N. SAWYER.
Seventh "	. .	" GEORGE G. STRATTON.
Eighth "	. .	" CHAS. O. BURRILL.
Ninth "	. .	" WM. H. PATTEE.
Tenth "	. .	" THOMAS F. TEMPLE.

On the staff of Eminent Commander Lotts were Eminent Sirs Samuel Mason, Jr., and John H. Upham, Past Commanders of Boston Commandery, and the following-named Eminent Sir Knights, members of the Massachusetts Union of Knights Templars Commanders, of which Eminent Commander Lotts is President, namely: Eminent Sir S. A. Bolster, Past Commander of Joseph Warren Commandery; Eminent Sir C. C. Bixby, Eminent Commander of Bay State Commandery; Eminent Sirs Baalis Sanford and Edward Parker, Jr., Past

Commanders of Bay State Commandery; Eminent Sir George W. Kingman, Eminent Commander of St. Omer Commandery; Eminent Sir Loring L. Fuller, Past Commander of Hugh De Payen Commandery; Eminent Sir Henry S. Bunton, Eminent Commander of Cyprus Commandery; and Eminent Sir E. H. Doolittle, Past Commander of William Parkman Commandery. Sir Charles E. Pierce, Senior Warden of St. Omer Commandery, was also upon the staff by invitation. The parade of the two Commands was through Dover and Washington Streets, Chester Square, Columbus Avenue and Berkeley Street to Odd Fellows' Hall, where an elegant banquet had been spread for the returned pilgrims. After seats had been taken, Eminent Commander Lotts called for order, and Prelate J. P. Bland asked a blessing. After a brief welcome from the Commander, the good things provided by Caterer Tufts were duly discussed, and then order was again restored by Eminent Commander Lotts, who gave as a toast to the guests of the occasion, "The De Molay Commandery — may the good fellowship existing now between its members and those of the Boston Commandery exist till time shall be no more." The Commander then called upon Sir Knight William H. Kent, Grand Commander of the Encampment of Massachusetts and Rhode Island, who spoke as follows:

GRAND COMMANDER KENT'S SPEECH.

Most Eminent Grand Commander, as I am here in the capacity of a welcomer rather than one who is to be welcomed, it gives me much pleasure to see you on such a joyous occasion as this. I wish I could find words adequate to express the feelings with which I and the Boston Commandery greet you here to-day, on your return from a pilgrimage, every step of which has seemed to be an ovation, during which I am glad to know that there has no casualty occurred, and from which you have all returned well and happy. [Applause.]

There will be those, at any rate, who have read accounts in the papers the last ten days, which have sneeringly asked why we dignify occasions of this character, and what there is, after all, so grand in Masonry. They say that we get together, and go through some secret performance and they do not know what, and that appears to be all that there is. Well, God bless them, they are not to blame for being ignorant on such a subject as Masonry. We only pray that they may yet receive further light, or have more charity till they do. But, in answer to some of these cavillers, I ask you what is the result of your pilgrimage? What have you brought back? Have you brought back a larger knowledge of men and things? Has humanity been broadened; your sensibilities quickened? Have you a higher respect for this grand old organization of ours? Do you come back with a determination to live more conscientiously its precepts. Aye; have you done anything to soften local differences, and allay political prejudices? Why, I hear the affirmative answer going up with a shout that makes the welkin ring! [Applause.] And has not your pilgrimage been a success in the best sense of the word? [Applause.] If anything is typified by this memorial day on which we meet —a day set apart to honor those who died in defence of the union of these States—if any principle is illustrated by your expedition and pilgrimage, it is the principle on which hangs all the law and the prophets: the principles of peace, love and good-will. The essential principle of Masonry has been the principle of Christianity. We want more of it; we want better to live it, and illustrate it. It is the thing that we have brought home with us. All we have from other great sources shall fail. Prophecy shall fail, tongues shall cease, knowledge shall vanish away; but Christian and Masonic love, charity and good-will, these shall all endure forever and forever. [Enthusiastic applause.] The things we glory in, the thing we feel reason to delight in, is love. The heavy burden under which we have been will one day from our weary shoulders move, and one thing alone shall remain : that thing is love. All beauty fades ; the lustre of human eyes grows dim ; the glories of nature pass away; and we hear only one voice, as one hears the sad farewell of a friend. There is only one sweet thing, and that is love. And when memory alone remains to us, and there is no refuge on a mother's knee for us who have grown old and sad with care and pain, brotherless and sisterless, on our way to that dark house from whence we shall not return, there is only one thing that hath no end; there is nothing but love. [Applause.] God bless us all, and make us wiser and purer and better for this thing. [Great applause.]

Following this address, the reorganized Temple Quartet — Messrs. George J. Parker, George W. Want, H. A. Cooke and A. C. Ryder — sang a selection, and then Eminent Commander F. G. Walbridge, of the De Molays, was introduced, and, after being greeted with three rousing cheers from the members of the Boston Command, briefly returned his thanks for the courtesies extended to the De Molays on their return home, saying that, though they were weary pilgrims travelling from afar, and over a route that had been but a series of ovations from the start, such a knightly greeting as that given by the Boston Command was sufficient to make all memories of fatigue vanish, and give renewed strength and vigor, by reason of the kindly feeling it exhibited between the two encampments. In closing he introduced Rev. Sir Knight Dadmun, prelate of the pilgrimage, who made one of his happiest efforts on this occasion. In returning thanks for the knightly greeting given this Commandery, the speaker said that though for the past ten days the De Molays had been welcomed and toasted on all occasions, none of these ovations had touched his heart as had that of the morning from the Boston Commandery, the mother of the De Molay. Calling for three cheers for the Boston Commandery, they were given with a will by the De Molays. Continuing, the speaker said: "You may judge that we have taken Richmond, but I assure you it is not so, for Richmond has captured us. Her challenge of three months ago was duly accepted, and the choice of time and place being given us, we chose May 19 and the city of Richmond, the weapon to be love. A fair day's fight was engaged in, and the conflict began. We felt, on a Thursday morning, when, without parade or ostentation, we decorated the monument of the Christian and hero, Stonewall Jackson — we felt that the battle was ours. Not so, however, for with redoubled exertions they renewed the contest and we were captured, but allowed to return home on parole, with orders to return again as soon as possible. So you see, Sir Knights, we are but prisoners of war, whipped out and out by the weapon of love." The speaker then recalled the events of the "pilgrimage," and the experiences of the pilgrims in the various cities, making a special reference to the fact that, in all the ovations, the women had been foremost, to him a conclusive evidence that the hearts of the brothers and fathers were in the words of welcome extended to the De Molays. Referring to the reception in New York, the speaker said: "The Sir Knights of Palestine Commandery are the liveliest set of men I ever met, and can get up more steam in five minutes than any engine in the universe." Here a "sky rocket" was given, a "fizz—boom—a—h" affair peculiar to the New York Commandery. In closing, the speaker said: "We had no idea of the welcome we should receive at the South, but we have had one of the most enjoyable times any set of boys ever had, and I feel as young as any of them." The quartet then sang again, and subsequently short but apt speeches were made by Generalissimo John L. Stevenson, Sir Knight Henry C. Barnabee, Sir Knight S. K. Rich, of the Palestine Commandery of New York, who announced that he had telegraphed his Commander that he had seen the De Molays safely home, Past Eminent Commander Wyzeman Marshall, of the Boston Commandery, Captain-General George F. Wright, of the De Molays, and Captain-General Edwin Wright, of the Boston Commandery. After the interchange of friendly greetings, the line of march was again formed, and the column proceeded to the soldiers' monument on the Common, where a halt was made, and Eminent Commander Walbridge, of the De Molay Commandery, placed the elegant floral offering of the Maryland Commandery of Baltimore upon the base of the statue, making this use of the tribute, in accordance with the general desire of the De Molay Commandery. The march was then resumed to Masonic Temple, where the line was dismissed, and the second pilgrimage to Richmond ended.

APPENDIX.

APPENDIX.

ROSTER — RICHMOND COMMANDERY, No. 2, K. T.

(*May 23, 1881.*)

Eminent Sir WM. T. ALLEN, *Commander.*
Sir I. S. TOWER, *Generalissimo*, elected Eminent Commander June 17.
" J. THOMPSON BROWN, *Captain-General*, elected Generalissimo June 17.
" J. F. MAYER, *Prelate*, elected Captain-General June 17.
" M. W. YARRINGTON, *Senior Warden*, elected Prelate June 17.
" JAS. H. CAPERS, *Junior Warden*, elected Senior Warden June 17.
" R. E. MACOMBER, *Treasurer*, re-elected Treasurer June 17.
" C. F. DANFORTH, *Recorder.*
" GEO. A. AINSLIE, *Standard Bearer*, re-appointed Standard Bearer June 17.
" A. R. COURTNEY, *Sword Bearer*, elected Junior Warden June 17.
" B. F. HOWARD, *Warder*, appointed Sword Bearer June 17.
" J. E. TYLER, ⎫ ⎧ appointed Warder June 17.
" CHAS. A. WEST, ⎬ *Guards*, ⎨ appointed Guard "
" W. ELLIS JONES, ⎭ ⎩
" D. B. COLLINS, *Captain of Guard*, re-appointed Captain of Guard June 17.

APPENDIX.

PAST COMMANDERS.

Eminent Sir L. L. BASS.
" " JOHN F. REGNAULT.
" " A. S. LEE.
" " JAS. A. SCOTT.

HONORARY MEMBERS.

EMINENT COMMANDER, }
GENERALISSIMO, } De Molay Commandery, Boston, Mass.
CAPTAIN-GENERAL, }

EMINENT COMMANDER, }
GENERALISSIMO, } St. John's Commandery, Providence, R. I.
CAPTAIN-GENERAL, }

Sir E. R. Cheney, De Molay Commandery, Boston.
" F. L. GILMAN, Cœur de Leon Commandery, Boston.
" JOHN SCOTT, Morton Commandery, New York.
" WM. ALLEN, Richmond Commandery, Richmond, Va.
" JAS. EVANS, Richmond Commandery, Richmond, Va.

SIR KNIGHTS.

Sir John Adam.
" A. A. Allen.
" Jas. W. Archer.
" Aug. Arsell, Jr.
" H. A. Atkinson.
" A. S. Bacon.
" D. G. Baker.
" Isbon Benedict.
" C. P. Bigger.
" W. W. Baldwin.

Sir I. D. Briggs.
" Geo. H. Bright.
" Francis J. Boggs.
" Alex. M. Brownell.
" Frank Barrows.
" Ro. Caruthers.
" J. A. Chambliss.
" Maurice Clagett.
" Geo. L. Clarke.
" R. N. Crooks.

APPENDIX. 113

Sir Thos. M. Cullingsworth.
" Wm. Cullingsworth.
" Judson Cunningham.
" Wm. Davis.
" P. S. Derbyshire.
" J. S. Dodson.
" R. H. Duesberry. Appointed Second Guard June 17.
" C. C. T. Duncker.
" John E. Edwards.
" Wm. Ellison.
" Maurice Evans.
" S. M. G. Fisher. Elected Recorder June 17.
" S. G. Flournoy.
" John Frey.
" W. J. Gentry. Appointed Third Guard June 17.
" John W. Gill.
" B. W. Gillis.
" W. H. Glasscock.
" Thos. H. Gunn.
" Jos. Hall.
" M. P. Handy.
" Chas. H. Harvey.
" B. C. Hartsoak.
" Geo. A. Hundley.
" Wm. B. Isaacs, Jr.
" S. B. Jacobs.
" C. C. Johnson.
" W. T. King.
" Shirley King.

Sir Wm. Krouse.
" R. T. Lacy.
" N. M. Lee.
" Wm. P. Lee.
" Chas. Lundin.
" John McFarland.
" A. C. Maynard.
" R. Maynard.
" John J. Montague.
" Alex. McRae.
" Henry T. Miller.
" John T. Moore.
" John E. Morris.
" Wm. A. Moss.
" Wm. Murray.
" John A. Netherland.
" Jones A. Otey.
" R. M. J. Paynter.
" H. L. Pelouze.
" Wetherill Peterson.
" John Perry.
" H. F. Phillips.
" Wm. C. Price.
" C. W. Purcell.
" Ro. E. Richardson.
" Wm. F. Richardson.
" Jas. L. Riddick.
" W. A. Robinson.
" John T. Rogers.
" Henry W. Rountree.
" Frank M. Sherry.
" E. H. Simpson.
" John T. Sizer.

Sir I. T. Smith.
" Ellis C. Stacy.
" J. M. Stevens.
" S. B. Sutherland.
" John I. Stevenson.
" Allen Talbatt.
" Chas. H. Talbatt.
" E. B. Taylor.
" H. Selden Taylor.
" Geo. C. Vanderslice.
" A. J. Vaughan.
" Henry Wall.

Sir Isaac N. Walker.
" G. A. Wallace.
" A. W. Weddell.
" O. F. Weisiger.
" W. H. Weisiger.
" A. B. Wells.
" W. T. West.
" Wm. E. Wiatt.
" J. R. Williams.
" John W. Wright.
" Wm. A. Wyatt.

ROSTER OF COMMANDERY OF ST. ANDREW, No. 13, OF RICHMOND, VIRGINIA.

(*May*, 1881.)

OFFICERS.

Eminent Sir THOMAS JEFFERSON EVANS, *Commander.*
Sir JOS. VIRGINIUS BIDGOOD, *Generalissimo.*
" JOHN JEFFERSON WRIGHT, *Captain-General.*
Rev. Sir WM. C. SCHAEFFER, *Prelate.*
Sir ELBERT CELLERS WALTHALL, *Senior Warden.*
" GEORGE WASHINGTON POE, *Junior Warden.*
" GEORGE BOARDMAN STEEL, *Treasurer.*
Right Eminent Sir WM. BRYAN ISAACS, *Recorder.*
Sir WM. OVERTON ENGLISH, *Standard Bearer.*

Sir HOWARD SWINEFORD, *Sword Bearer.*
" WM. M. NETHERLAND, *Warder.*
" DENNIS B. COLLINS, *Captain Guard.*

PAST COMMANDERS.

Right Eminent WM. BRYAN ISAACS, *Past Grand Commander.*
Eminent WM. ELAM TANNER.

MEMBERS.

A. G. Babcock.
C. W. P. Brock.
John P. Bargamin.
Henry Bochmer.
A. B. Bigelow.
Henry Bodeker.
R. W. Bidgood.
L. D. Crenshaw, Jr.
James D. Crump.
Luther D. Camp.
E. A. Chalkley.
Samuel D. Davies.
Frank D. Dunlop.
Rev. Geo. W. Dame, Jr.
F. C. Ebell.
A. L. Fugua.
A. W. Garber.
Joseph F. Gibson.
R. H. M. Harrison.
John R. Johnson.
John E. Laughton, Jr.

Henry W. Murray.
Oscar M. Marshall.
Warner Moore.
C. W. Macfarlane.
N. C. Newton.
E. T. Parham.
James D. Patton.
J. W. Penick.
George W. Robinson.
Wm. D. Rice.
R. B. Swead.
Frank D. Steger.
George P. Stacy.
Jo. Lane Stern.
W. Hamilton Sands.
Edgar D. Taylor.
James T. Vaughan.
Charles E. Wortham.
Samuel B. Witt.
G. Waddy Wilde.

ROSTER OF ST. JOHN'S COMMANDERY, No. 1.

Sir Geo. H. Rhodes, *Eminent Commander.*
" Jas. C. Lester, *Generalissimo.*
" G. L. Shepley, *Captain-General.*
Eminent Sir A. H. Cushman, *Prelate.*
Sir Pardon Wilbur, *Senior Warden.*
" Jno. Heathcote, *Junior Warden.*
" Jno. G. Massie, *Treasurer.*
" Wm. H. Perry, *Recorder.*
" C. M. Sheldon, *Sword Bearer.*
" W. C. Hammond, *Standard Bearer.*
" D. B. Davis, *Warder.*

GUARDS.

Jno. M. Buffinton. W. H. Sherman.
W. A. Wheaton.

PAST EMINENT COMMANDERS.

Eminent Sir Newton D. Arnold.
" W. E. Husband.
" Geo. H. Burnham.
" Stillman White.

SIR KNIGHTS.

Sir T. F. Arnold.   Sir A. Coville.
" G. M. Ardoene.   " H. A. Claflin.
" A. L. Bliss.   " R. Chadwick.
" J. E. Brown.   " A. B. Gardiner.
" J. H. Belcher.   " C. E. Harris.
" G. F. Battey.   " J. G. Hastings.
" W. R. Bodfish.   " R. H. Hall.
" C. E. Bourne.   " B. F. Kingsbury.

APPENDIX.

Sir C. Law.
" C. Lawton.
" C. Monsell.
" O. M. Mitchell.
" M. Ogden.
" J. G. Pearce.
" W. F. Dillaby.
" D. N. Davis.
" P. S. Dobson.
" H. B. Dexter.
" C. H. Dunham.
" L. H. Eddy.
" T. D. Elsbree.
" J. R. Fales.
" G. M. Freeborn.

Sir G. Fuller.
" C. Gorton.
" T. M. Rounds.
" F. J. Rice.
" S. D. Spink.
" S. B. Swan.
" A. Thompson.
" L. H. Tillinghast.
" J. F. Utton.
" J. A. Whaley.
" W. L. Walker.
" P. T. Washburn.
" Ira Winsor.
" W. R. Walker.

LADIES.

Mrs. Jno. Heathcote.
" Chas. Monsell.
Miss Mattie Gorton.
Mrs. A. Waterman.
Miss F. Waterman.
Mrs. N. D. Arnold.
" J. C. Lester.
" A. L. Bliss.
Miss Ella Bliss.
" Anna Copeland.
Mrs. J. E. Brown.
" W. L. Walker.
" S. D. Spink.
Mrs. T. F. Arnold.

Mrs. C. Law.
" P. Wilbur.
" S. White.
Miss A. White.
Mrs. C. J. Pullen.
" S. B. Swan.
" C. H. Dunham.
" A. Thompson.
" W. H. Sherman.
" J. G. Hastings.
" A. Coville.
" F. J. Rice.
" O. M. Mitchell.

Fraternal Greetings to Columbia Commandery, No. 2, from De Molay Commandery of Boston.

In Memoriam.

SIR JAMES ABRAM GARFIELD, late President of the United States, was shot and mortally wounded by an assassin in the city of Washington, July 2, 1881, and, after suffering intensely for nearly eighty days, with that cheerful Christian fortitude which added the crowning lustre to his great and beautifully rounded character, departed this life, September 19, aged forty-nine years and ten months, and was buried at Cleveland, Ohio, September 26, 1881.

Princes and rulers in all parts of the world delighted to honor him, during his great sufferings, with telegrams of heart-felt sympathy, and fervent prayers for his recovery; and when he died the civilized world was draped in mourning. It is generally conceded that no chief magistrate, of this or any other nation, ever died so universally esteemed and beloved as was our brother and Sir Knight, whose life and death we now commemorate by dedicating these pages to his memory.

We, as a Commandery of Knights Templars, have special reasons for recording our high appreciation of his knightly courtesy, which was extended to us when we were passing through the Capital on a pilgrimage to Richmond, only six weeks before he was assassinated. On arriving at Washington, May 20, in company with St. John's Commandery of Providence, we were royally received by the Knights Templars of the city, including Columbia Commandery, No. 2, of which President Garfield was a member, and by his kindness the five Commanderies in line were admitted within the grounds in front of the White House, and were reviewed by him. The next day he personally received and cordially greeted us within the Executive Mansion. His noble, manly form, as he stood before us on that occasion, and the hearty shake of his generous hand, are reminiscences which can never be effaced.

We recommend the adoption of the following resolutions:

Resolved, That we hereby express our profound sorrow that our dear brother, Sir James Abram Garfield, should be cut down by the hand of a political fanatic in a time of peace, and so soon after he had obtained the loftiest position in the gift of his country. And yet we rejoice that he has not lived in vain. His calm resoluteness, his undaunted perseverance, his native dignity, his consistent demeanor, his unsullied integrity, his faith in God and his hope in immortality will remain a rich legacy for his family, our Fraternity, and the nation he honored and loved so well.

Resolved, That we tender the venerable mother, the devoted wife and the bereaved children our deep and tender sympathy; and we devoutly pray that the same noble, Christian fortitude, which was manifested by Mrs. Garfield during the trials and sufferings of her beloved husband, and which has made her name illustrious in all the world, may continue to support her in the multiplied cares and sorrows which must press heavily upon her.

Resolved, That we send mournful, and yet cordial greetings to our Fraters of Columbia Commandery, No. 2, and sincerely condole with them the irreparable loss of the renowned Hero, Statesman and Freemason, Sir James Abram Garfield, President of the United States.

Signed by the members of the Council and Committee, and attested by the Recorder under the seal of the Commandery.

BOSTON, October 19, 1882.

COMPLIMENTARY TESTIMONIAL

TO

RICHMOND COMMANDERY, No. 2, K. T.,

OF RICHMOND, VA.,

FROM DE MOLAY COMMANDERY, K. T., OF BOSTON, MASS.

WHEREAS, In response to a very cordial invitation extended to them by Richmond Commandery, No. 2, and the Commandery of St. Andrew, No. 13, both of Richmond, Virginia, the De Molay Commandery of Boston visited the city of Richmond, May 23, 1881, and were entertained with that knightly hospitality for which their Fraters of Virginia are justly celebrated, therefore,

Resolved, That we hereby tender the Sir Knights of Richmond our sincere and hearty thanks for the princely manner in which they received us, and the unbounded hospitality so magnanimously extended to us and our ladies, during the four days we sojourned in that beautiful city; and that our former high estimate of Southern hospitality, created by the most intimate fraternal relations between Knights Templars of Richmond and Boston, extending over a period of twenty-three years, has been more than realized; and the new members of our Commandery, who accompanied us on this second pilgrimage, substantially declare, "The half was never told."

Resolved, That the elegant and costly Knights Templars' sword, presented to De Molay Commandery by our Richmond Sir Knights, surpasses anything of the kind we have ever had the pleasure of receiving ; and that words are inadequate to express the gratitude we feel for this golden pledge of knightly courtesy and brotherly affection. Its keen, bright and beautiful blade will remind us of the valor, heroism and knightly chivalry of the donors; and we hereby pledge our sacred honor, as Knights Templars, that while we shall preserve it with jealous, loving care, it shall consume with rust rather than be drawn in the cause of injustice and oppression.

Resolved, That we hereby express our heart-felt gratitude to his Excellency, Governor F. W. M. Holliday, his Honor, Mayor W. C. Carrington, and Sir A. R. Courtney, for their noble, fraternal and patriotic ad dresses of welcome at the GRAND RECEPTION, May 24th; and to all the citizens — especially the ladies — for the genial, loving and magnanimous peals of welcome with which we were received and greeted everywhere, amid elaborate and gorgeous decorations, and the distribution of wreaths, crowns and bouquets of beautiful flowers; for the opportunities afforded us of visiting their happy homes and places of historic interest, not only in the city but along the banks of the majestic James, one of the noblest rivers in America, also the factories and places of commercial interest; and for the many and various *souvenirs* given us as tokens of woman's love and man's noble generosity.

Resolved, That hereafter the twenty-sixth of May, the day on which the GRAND BANQUET was given, be observed by De Molay Commandery as an anniversary, in commemoration of our late pilgrimage to Richmond.

Signed by the members of the Council and Committee, and attested by the Recorder under the seal of the Commandery.

COMPLIMENTARY TESTIMONIAL
TO THE
COMMANDERY OF ST. ANDREW, No. 13, K. T.,
OF RICHMOND, VA.,
FROM DE MOLAY COMMANDERY, K. T., OF BOSTON, MASS.

WHEREAS, In response to a very cordial invitation extended to them by the Commandery of St. Andrew, No. 13, and Richmond Commandery, No. 2, both of Richmond, Virginia, the De Molay

Commandery of Boston visited the City of Richmond, May 23, 1881, and were entertained with that knightly hospitality for which their Fraters of Virginia are justly celebrated, therefore,

Resolved, That we hereby tender the Sir Knights of Richmond our sincere and hearty thanks for the princely manner in which they received us, and the unbounded hospitality so magnanimously extended to us and our ladies, during the four days we sojourned in that beautiful city; and that our former high estimate of Southern hospitality, created by the most intimate fraternal relations between Knights Templars of Richmond and Boston, extending over a period of twenty-three years, has been more than realized; and the new members of our Commandery, who accompanied us on this second pilgrimage, substantially declare, "The half was never told."

Resolved, That the elegant and costly Knights Templars' sword, presented to De Molay Commandery by our Richmond Sir Knights, surpasses anything of the kind we have ever had the pleasure of receiving; and that words are inadequate to express the gratitude we feel for this golden pledge of knightly courtesy and brotherly affection. Its keen, bright and beautiful blade will remind us of the valor, heroism and knightly chivalry of the donors; and we hereby pledge our sacred honor, as Knights Templars, that while we shall preserve it with jealous, loving care, it shall consume with rust rather than be drawn in the cause of injustice and oppression.

Resolved, That we hereby express our heart felt gratitude to his Excellency, Governor F. W. M. Holliday, his Honor, Mayor W. C. Carrington, and Sir A. R. Courtney, for their noble, fraternal and patriotic addresses of welcome at the GRAND RECEPTION, May 24, and to all the citizens — especially the ladies — for the genial, loving and magnanimous peals of welcome with which we were received and greeted everywhere, amid elaborate and gorgeous decorations, and the distribution of wreaths, crowns and bouquets of beautiful flowers; for the opportunities afforded us of visiting their happy homes and places of historic interest, not only in the city but along the banks of the majestic James, one of the noblest rivers in America, also the factories and places of commercial interest; and for the many and various *souvenirs* given us as tokens of woman's love and man's noble generosity.

Resolved, That hereafter the twenty-sixth of May, the day on which the GRAND BANQUET was given, be observed by De Molay Commandery as an anniversary, in commemoration of our late pilgrimage to Richmond.

Signed by the members of the Council and Committee, and attested by the Recorder under the seal of the Commandery.

De Molay Commandery of Knights Templars of Boston, Mass., in conclave assembled, sendeth knightly greeting to their Fraters of Fredericksburg Commandery No. 1.

We greet you from grateful hearts, and minds crowded with pleasant recollections of the courtesies extended to us and our ladies, by the Sir Knights and citizens of your city, upon the occasion of our brief visit on the twenty-third of May, 1881. Our recent pilgrimage to Richmond was a continued ovation from the time we arrived in Washington until we returned home, and while it would be as impossible as it is unnecessary to state where we were most cordially received and royally entertained, we can truly say that during the few hours we were permitted to be your guests, and partake of your unbounded hospitality, impressions were made upon the mind and heart of each one who participated that time can never efface. It was, indeed, a bright and sunny spot in life, to which our minds will revert with ever-increasing delight. We remember with peculiar pleasure that this was our first stop in the Old Dominion, which was so intimately associated with our own beloved Commonwealth in those early historic events that gave to each immortal renown. We shall always recall with delight the knightly bearing of your Commandery as you received and escorted us through your principal streets, so beautifully and tastefully decorated, and thronged with people who manifested such friendly interest that we felt we were among friends and brothers. Our hearts burned within us as we listened to the eloquent address of Judge Goolrick, assuring us of a cordial welcome to your hearts and homes. We remember his soul-stirring sentiments of patriotism and Masonic truth, that made us realize, as perhaps never before, that although we are citizens of different States, we are one people, joint-heirs of a glorious past, and marching together "in the foremost files of time," animated by the same lofty purposes and hopes for our common country. As we stood in sight of the grave of the mother who gave birth to him who was "first in the hearts of his countrymen," and realized that we were surrounded by the scenes that inspired and delighted his boyhood, and that here he commenced his Masonic career, we felt that, like the templars of ancient times, we had made a pilgrimage to a sacred spot; that we were upon holy ground.

We shall never forget the rare social pleasure we enjoyed at the residence of Eminent Commander R. S. Chew, and the elegant, refreshing and bountiful entertainment we then received; nor the delightful manner in which it was served by the fair maidens and charming matrons of Fredericksburg, who, by their grace and loveliness, contributed so much to our happiness.

Dear Sir Knights of Fredericksburg, for all these kind attentions we thank you sincerely and heartily, and, through you, all who contributed to the pleasures of that occasion, and we trust the friendships there so firmly established may be still further cemented, and last "till time with us shall be no more."

With all our hearts we add our mother tongue's best benison — God bless you, one and all.

Signed by the members of the Council and Committee, and attested by the Recorder under the seal of the Commandery.

COMPLIMENTARY TESTIMONIAL

TO

DE MOLAY MOUNTED COMMANDERY,

No. 4, K. T.,

OF WASHINGTON, D. C.

FROM DE MOLAY COMMANDERY, K. T., BOSTON, MASS.

WHEREAS, In response to a fraternal invitation extended to them by De Molay Mounted Commandery, No. 4, the De Molay Commandery of Boston visited the city of Washington on the twentieth and twenty-first of May, 1881, and were most hospitably entertained, therefore,

Resolved, That we hereby tender the officers and members of De Molay Mounted Commandery, No. 4, of Washington, our hearty thanks, for their princely reception and generous hospitality; and that our warm attachment to the Knights Templars of the Capital, created by the most intimate fraternal relations in years gone by, has been greatly strengthened by the knightly courtesy and generosity manifested toward us and our ladies during our visit to that city.

Resolved, That their presentation of an elegant photograph of the Capitol is hereby gratefully acknowledged, and that it be placed in our armory as a memento of the unbounded liberality and kindness of the De Molays of Washington.

Resolved, That we hereby express our profound gratitude to the President of the United States, Sir JAMES A. GARFIELD, for his knightly courtesy, in reviewing the Knights Templars during their parade; and also for personally receiving and greeting us and our ladies within the Executive Mansion; and that we tender our sincere thanks to the officers of the Government Departments for the great pleasure they afforded us by escorting us through many of the public buildings.

Finally, our De Molay Fraters of Washington, ever mindful of what is appropriate as well as generous, concluded the festivities by giving us a delightful sail down the Potomac River to Mount Vernon, where rest, in honor and glory, the remains of the renowned hero, statesman and FREEMASON, GEORGE WASHINGTON. As our feet pressed the soil of the home of the "Father of his Country," we could but reflect upon his spotless character, and resolve to imitate his many virtues as the highest tribute we could pay to the memory of this distinguished and eminent patron of Freemasonry. For all these social and intellectual feasts, we say to our noble brothers, God bless you!

Signed by the members of the Council and Committee, and attested by the Recorder under the seal of the Commandery.

DE MOLAY COMMANDERY OF KNIGHTS TEMPLARS,
BOSTON, September 28, 1881.
To the Most Eminent Commander, Officers and Sir Knights of Beauseant Commandery of Knights Templars, No. 8, Baltimore, Md.— Greeting:

WHEREAS, The committee appointed by De Molay Commandery, to prepare and forward to Beauseant Commandery of Baltimore, Md., an expression of their appreciation of the knightly courtesies and attentions shown to them during their recent sojourn in your beautiful city, in May last, take great pleasure in submitting the following :

Resolved, That De Molay Commandery most respectfully tenders to the noble-hearted Fraters of the celebrated Beauseant Commandery, and also to all other participating Commanderies, their sincere thanks and grateful appreciation for the unbounded hospitality extended to them upon their reception within the walls of your beautiful monumental city.

Resolved, That we shall look back with pride to the magnificent escort with which you honored us, and the remembrance of the march through your beautiful streets, headed by such an elegant body of Knights Templars, will ever remain one of the brightest scenes of our pilgrimage. The brilliant reception in the evening, where eloquent words of welcome, by your esteemed Commander and honored Mayor, sent a thrill of joy through our hearts that time will never efface ; where beautiful ladies, inspiring music and delicate viands, all in perfect harmony, told the same story, that we were indeed among friends and true "Soldiers of the Cross."

Resolved, That by your attention to us you have but maintained that part of the symbolic meaning of your name "Beauseant" — "Fair and pleasant to Christians" — and that we await an early opportunity of reciprocating your knightly hospitality and attention.

Signed by the members of the Council and Committee, and attested by the Recorder under the seal of the Commandery.

DE MOLAY COMMANDERY OF KNIGHTS TEMPLARS,

BOSTON, September 28, 1881.

To the Eminent Commander, Officers and Sir Knights of Palestine Commandery of Knights Templars, No. 18, New York, — Greeting:

De Molay Commandery of Knights Templars desiring to acknowledge through their Committee, in a formal manner, their appreciation of your unlimited and generous entertainment, during their brief sojourn in the great Metropolis of America, beg leave to submit the following

PREAMBLE AND RESOLUTIONS.

WHEREAS, On the afternoon of May 28, 1881, a body of Knights Templars arrived on the confines of your beautiful dominion, weary and worn with well-doing; they were returning to their humble homes, in the far East, after a long and arduous pilgrimage to the Mecca of their affection, the fair Virginia, where, like Knights of old, they had journeyed to offer their orisons and renew their vows.

"Weary pilgrims" as they were, they were taken in charge by a detachment of your guards, and conducted across the river, and delivered up as prisoners to your command. Fain would they have rebelled, but when they beheld the spotless raiment of their captors they said among themselves, this must indeed be a band of angels sent to conduct us to the gates of Palestine. One and and all proclaimed: "Lead on, in such company we will follow even unto the gates of death."

The line of march was immediately taken up, and we were conducted through streets and avenues teeming with the busy cares of daily life. Little did we heed them, but with renewed vigor, under the influence of the most inspiring music, we pressed onward under the leadership of our captors, until finally we arrived at the outer gate of the Temple. Up, up they led us, through long and narrow defiles, until at last we arrived within their Asylum, when the rattle of musketry, the boom of artillery, and the sh— of sky-rockets, told us plainer than words that we were not their prisoners, but honored guests.

In less time than it takes to record the fact, the cares and fatigues of our pilgrimage were forgotten in the jovial good fellowship of our new found

Fraters, the Knights of Palestine, who were unremitting in their attention to our personal wants and comfort. The delicate compliment paid to our ladies in the reception by the ladies of Palestine Commandery, at the St. Nicholas Hotel, and so ably carried out by its popular proprietor, constituted one of the brightest little episodes of our entire pilgrimage.

Untiring in their devotion to our welfare while in New York, they were not satisfied with welldoing, and sent with us, as a guard of honor, Sir Knights Rich and Whitman, to see that we reached safely our homes. Immediately upon our arrival these Sir Knights delivered us up to Boston Commandery, and telegraphed their Eminent Commander that they had delivered their guests to Boston Commandery, and that they had faithfully discharged their duty. Such devotion we had not dreamed of, and we are under deep and lasting obligations to them.

We came as strangers, but we departed feeling that we had left behind a band of true, noblehearted Knights and Brothers, and the recollections of the social hours that we enjoyed with them will remain forever one of the brightest pages in our lives as Knights Templar.

Resolved, That the sincere thanks of De Molay Commandery be extended to our Fraters of Palestine Commandery, for the elegant and hospitable manner in which they honored us as their guests while passing through their city.

Resolved, That a petition from De Molay Commandery be forwarded to Palestine Commandery, No. 18, of New York, craving permission to use their copyrighted "Sky-Rocket," upon our paying a suitable royalty.

Resolved, That the Knights of De Molay Commandery look forward with a great deal of pleasure to the time when it may be their privilege to welcome the Knights of Palestine within their Asylum, and return, in the bonds of Knighthood, the elegant reception with which they honored us.

Signed by the members of the Council and Committee, and attested by the Recorder under the seal of the Commandery.

To the Eminent Commander, Officers and Sir Knights of Boston Commandery, Knights Templars, — Greeting:

De Molay Commandery Knights Templars, Boston, duly appreciating the Knightly courtesy of Boston Commandery, K. T., extended to them on the occasion of their return from their pilgrimage to Richmond, Virginia, May 30, 1881, appointed on June 22, 1881, a Committee to prepare a suitable testimonial in recognition of the same, when the said Committee submitted the following preamble and resolutions, and they were unanimously adopted.

WHEREAS, Boston Commandery, in continuation of the friendly relations which have so long existed between them and De Molay Commandery, has again shown in a highly creditable manner the knightly courtesy which shows them to be true Soldiers of the Cross, therefore,

Resolved, That the heart-felt thanks of De Molay Commandery be and are hereby extended to the Fraters of Boston Commandery, for the very cordial reception given by them to our "Weary Pilgrims travelling from afar."

Resolved, That we shall ever cherish with grateful hearts, the kind words and noble sentiments so feelingly and eloquently expressed at the generous banquet provided for us on that occasion.

Resolved, That by this expression of fraternal regard, Boston Commandery has bound us to them with new chains, and it shall ever be our desire to reciprocate their kind greeting so magnanimously extended.

Signed by the members of the Council and Committee, and attested by the Recorder under the seal of the Commandery.

SOUVENIRS FOR SOUTHERN KNIGHTS.

Since the return of the De Molay Commandery of Knights Templars from its Richmond pilgrimage, its members have been anxious to send their Fraters of the Southern cities then visited, some

souvenir which should keep constantly in the
minds of their hosts at Washington, Fredericksburg and Richmond the memory of the pleasant
events of their stay with them in May last. Such
souvenirs have been at last made ready, and last
evening, through the courtesy of Capt. Lovering, of
the Adams express, they were forwarded by special
messenger to their destination. The souvenirs
consist of elegant swords, designed for the use of
the Eminent Commander of the Richmond, No. 2,
and St. Andrew's, No. 13, Commands of Richmond,
the Fredericksburg Command of Fredericksburg,
and the mounted De Molay Command of Wash
ington, to be worn during the term of office, and
then to be presented to successive incumbents in
perpetuity. The swords were made by the Ames
Company, and are pronounced to be the finest
specimens ever made in this country. The handles
of the weapons are of ivory, with a mounted Templar beautifully etched in colors on one side, and
the Maltese cross of the Order on the other, the
top of the hilt consisting of a helmeted head. The
cross hilt has the triangle of the Order in enamel
at either end, with twelve jewels in each, and the
guard is ornamented with a bas-relief of a Templar
stretched before his tent gazing upon the cross in
the sky. The diamond-pointed blade is etched in
gold and silver with the name of the Commandery
on one side, and the scene of the temple and camp
on the other. The scabbard is of gold, ornamented
with bas-reliefs of the cross and crown upon the

upper escutcheon, and of the pilgrim on his way on the lower escutcheon, the engraved monogram of each Command occupying the space between the two. A De Molay belt of black velvet and gold lace ornaments, mounted with three belt slides and gold barrel chains, accompanied each sword, and each of these elegant souvenirs was packed in a black walnut case, with blue satin linings and pads. Letters were forwarded to the several Commanderies tendering the souvenirs, which were received on Washington's Birthday, the event intended to be commemorated by the presentations.

The committee appointed by De Molay Commandery to procure the swords and present them to their Southern Fraters, consisted of Eminent Sir J. W. Dadmun, Sir William B. Fisher and Sir F. J. Davis. The following presentation letters, duly attested by the Committee, accompanied the swords:

BOSTON, February 22, 1882.

To the Eminent Commander, Officers and Members of Richmond Commandery, No. 2, Richmond, Va.:

Dear Brothers and Sir Knights,— Although some nine months have passed since the De Molays made their second pilgrimage to Richmond, rest assured that no length of time can diminish in the least degree the bond of union existing between them and their noble Fraters of Virginia. And as an enduring testimony of our gratitude to you for your unbounded knightly hospitality, and as a token of our constant love and good fellowship, we now forward to you a Commander's sword, and a De Molay belt, hoping that each presiding Commander will wear them within your Asylum in memory of the De Molays of Boston. We beg you to accept them; not so much for their intrinsic value as for the knightly friendship and affection of the donors.

To us all, as Knights Templars, the sword has a moral significance that makes it beautifully appropriate, for in our hands as Knights Templars it becomes endowed with three excellent qualities: "Its hilt by faith, its blade by hope, and its point by mercy;" three glorious attributes, which, when possessed by the human heart, make the perfect man. Faith in God, hope in immortality and charity to all mankind is the practical faith on which Templar Masonry is founded. May the happy union formed between the Sir Knights of Richmond and Boston in 1858 be perpetuated until faith shall be lost in sight, and hope shall end in full fruition.

In the name of De Molay Commandery of Boston this sword and belt are hereby presented to Richmond Commandery, No. 2, of Richmond, Virginia, on this anniversary of the birthday of the renowned Freemason and Father of his Country— Virginia's noblest sire — GEORGE WASHINGTON.

BOSTON, February 22, 1882.

To the Eminent Commander, Officers and Members of the Commandery of St. Andrew, No. 13, Richmond, Virginia:

Dear Brothers and Sir Knights,—It seems but a day since the De Molays of Boston were with the valiant Templars of Richmond. All the events of the splendid ovation given to the visiting Sir Knights are full of thrilling interest, and memory recalls them with a vividness which is almost transporting. Our expectations were more than realized, and the second pilgrimage of De Molay Commandery to the "Old Dominion," last May, was made, by the generous, knightly hospitality of the Richmond Sir Knights, one of the greatest events of its history.

> "Long, long be my heart with such memories filled!
> Like the vase in which roses have once been distilled;
> You may break, you may ruin the vase, if you will,
> But the scent of the roses will hang round it still."

As one of the four Commanderies which formed the solid square on that occasion, St. Andrew should also receive the honors and awards of valiant Templars. Therefore, as a testimony of our gratitude for your knightly hospitality, and as a token of our constant love and good fellowship, we now forward to you a Commander's sword and a De Molay belt, hoping that each presiding Commander will wear them within the Asylum, in memory of the De Molays of Boston. We beg you to accept them; not so much for their intrinsic value as for the knightly friendship and affection of the donors.

In the name of De Molay Commandery of Boston this sword and belt are hereby presented to the Commandery of St. Andrew, No. 13, of Richmond, Virginia, on this anniversary of the birthday of the renowned Freemason and Father of his Country—Virginia's noblest sire— GEORGE WASHINGTON.

BOSTON, February 22, 1882.

To the Eminent Commander, Officers and Members of Fredericksburg Commandery, No. 1, Fredericksburg, Virginia:

Dear Brothers and Sir Knights,—On the twenty-third of May last, the De Molay Commandery of Boston, in company with St. John's Commandery of Providence, entered the "Old Dominion," on a pilgrimage to Richmond. Having previously accepted a very kind and cordial invitation from you to visit Fredericksburg on the way, we were greatly surprised to find, on arriving there, that not only the Knights Templars but the citizens had turned out *en masse* to give us a grand reception and a hearty welcome. The booming of cannon, the waving of banners, the floral decorations and appropriate mottoes, the sumptuous banquet in the beautiful grove surrounding the lovely home of

Eminent Commander Chew, and, above all, the hearty greetings of the Templars, the citizens and the ladies, made the "pilgrims" feel that their lines had indeed fallen unto them in pleasant places.

And what could be more appropriate than for a society of Masons, in making a pilgrimage to the Capital of Old Virginia, to visit the place where George Washington first received Masonic light, and where sleeps his sainted mother beneath the sacred soil of the "First Colony of Virginia?" We assure you that the few hours we spent in your city, so full of historic interest, and with a people so abounding in their hospitality, will be in our history like "apples of gold in pictures of silver," and fond memory will often recall them with transporting joy and gladness.

As a slight testimony of our high appreciation of the ovation given us on that occasion, and as a token of our love and knightly fellowship, we now forward to you a Commander's sword and a De Molay belt, to be worn by each presiding Commander within the Asylum, in memory of the De Molays of Boston. We hope you will accept them as a souvenir of the knightly friendship and affection of the donors. True friendship can never be bought with gold, but

> "The friends thou hast, and their adoption tried,
> Grapple them by the soul with hooks of steel."

In the name of De Molay Commandery of Boston, this sword and belt are hereby presented to

Fredericksburg Commandery, No. 1, of Fredericksburg, Virginia, on this anniversary of the birthday of the renowned Freemason and "Father of his Country"—Virginia's noblest sire—GEORGE WASHINGTON.

BOSTON, February 22, 1882.

To the Eminent Commander, Officers and Members of De Molay Mounted Commandery, No. 4, of Washington, D. C.:

Dear Brothers and Sir Knights,—The members of De Molay Commandery of Boston, who made a second pilgrimage to Richmond last May, will never forget the cordial greetings with which they were received by the Sir Knights of Washington, and especially the princely ovation given them by De Molay Mounted Commandery, No. 4.

The grand reception given us as we entered the Capital, the march through the beautiful streets, the review and reception given by our late and beloved President, SIR JAMES A. GARFIELD, the social levee, the carriage ride, the sail on the majestic Potomac, and the visit to Mount Vernon, in a word, *all* the incidents of our two days sojourn with the De Molays of Washington, afforded the "pilgrims" unspeakable pleasure, and will ever be to them "the consolation to memory dear."

"There are moments of life that we never forget,
  Which brighten and brighten as time steals away,
  They give a new charm to the happiest lot,
  And they shine on the gloom of the lonelicst day."

As an enduring testimony of our gratitude for your unbounded, knightly hospitality, and as a memento of our constant love and good fellowship, we now forward to you a Commander's sword and a De Molay belt, hoping that each presiding Commander will wear them within the Asylum, in memory of the De Molays of Boston. We beg you to accept them as a pledge of the knightly courtesy and friendship of the donors.

In behalf of De Molay Commandery of Boston, and on this anniversary of the birthday of the renowned Freemason and Father of his Country, GEORGE WASHINGTON, this sword and belt are hereby presented to the De Molay Mounted Commandery, No. 4, of Washington, D. C.

LETTERS OF ACKNOWLEDGMENT.

RICHMOND, June 6, 1882.

Eminent Sir J. W. DADMUN, *Sir* WM. B. FISHER, *and Sir* F. J. DAVIS, *Committee, Boston, Mass.:*

Dear Sir Knights, — At the regular assembly of their Commandery held on Tuesday night last, the twenty-eighth ultimo, the undersigned were appointed a committee to return the acknowledgments and thanks of Richmond Commandery, No. 2, to you and the Sir Knights of De Molay Commandery, for your courteous and kind letter, and the beautiful and elegant present sent them. This evidence was not needed, Sir Knights, to assure us that we were not forgotten by our beloved Fraters of De Molay; but it is duly appreciated by us, and we will keep and cherish it, as a token of the high regard and affectionate esteem existing between De Molay and Richmond, No. 2, and which we prize beyond measure. No meeting of the members of Richmond Commandery is ever held that some incident of our pilgrimage to Boston, or your pilgrimage to Richmond, and some pleasurable experience connected therewith, is not related, *and the story of our loves never grows old.*

The sword and belt shall be worn, dear friends, as you desire, and our assemblies will have additional interest and pleasure from the presence of this constant reminder of the affectionate remembrance of the De Molays, and henceforth each newly created Templar in Richmond Commandery, No. 2, shall receive from its blade the inspiration of the knightly deeds and chivalric courtesy and bearing of the donors. In the name of, and for Richmond Commandery, No. 2, we thank you for the elegant and valuable present, but more than, and above, all, for the touching sentiments of your letter, which have gone to our hearts.

Truly and fraternally yours,

LUCIEN L. BASS,
WM. T. ALLEN,   } *Committee.*
J. THOMPSON BROWN,

RICHMOND, VA., February 25, 1882.
Sirs J. W. DADMUN, WM. B. FISHER, *and* F. J. DAVIS, *Committee:*

It has been said, dear Sir Knights, that "there are three friendships which are beneficial: Friendship with the upright, friendship with the sincere and friendship with the man of observation." Such are the elements of the friendship which has bound the Templars of Massachusetts and Virginia for more than a generation. It was in the spring of 1881 that that friendship culminated — between De Molay and St. Andrew — in the elements of that mutual love which is an "emblem of eternity, confounding all idea of time, effacing all memory of a beginning and banishing all fear of an ending."

Last night, at a regular assembly of the Commandery of St. Andrew, there was presented to it, on behalf of De Molay Commandery, a "Commander's sword and a De Molay belt," as a testimony of their "constant love and friendship." *We*, of the present generation, require no outward, visible sign to remind *us* of the ties which bind *us*, but, we receive and accept, with grateful emotions, this beautiful tribute of affection, to hand down to our successors, that they who were not participants in the joys of 1875 and 1881 may have before them, and in their constant service, a memorial of our associations and ties; and as each is constituted, dubbed and created a Knight

Templar, may this testimonial, under whose application he is made a member of our household, carry with it a knowledge and appreciation of the ties of affectionate Brotherhood which now bind De Molay and St. Andrew, and thus transmit them from generation to generation, throughout all time.

On behalf of "the Commandery of St. Andrew, No. 13," we are,

Fraternally yours,

WM. E. TANNER, ⎫
WM. B. ISAACS,   ⎬ *Committee.*
J. V. BIDGOOD,   ⎭

FREDERICKSBURG, VA., March 3, 1882.

To the Eminent Commander, Officers and Members of De Molay Commandery, Boston, Mass.:

Sir Knights,—Words fail us to express the pleasurable feelings and grateful emotions awakened by the "token of your love and knightly fellowship—a Commander's sword and a De Molay belt," with its accompanying words of "brotherly love," which we have recently received. It needed not this handsome gift to assure us of your appreciation of the slight act of hospitality it pleased us to tender you, for the expression of your gratification while with us more than repaid us for the little we did for your refreshment "while travelling from afar;" and now, since you have reiterated your gratification in such an expressive manner, we have been made to realize, "It is more blessed to give than to receive."

However, we beg to assure you, Sir Knights and Fraters, that above the intrinsic worth of your gift is its extrinsic value. The feelings which prompted the gift, the friendship it exhibits, the desire on your part to bind us to yourselves in lasting bonds of brotherhood, all unite to make us realize a gift is invaluable, whatever it may be, when it is the outward expression of the heart's noblest impulses.

We are reminded by this token very vividly of the characteristic of your people, to turn the tables and make your creditors debtors. Boston has ever been noted for the culture and refinement of her citizens, and therefore to win their favor is an honor to be desired; and we have the evidence now before our eyes that some of its representatives, in the persons of the members of your Commandery, with a splendid generosity, have honored their old city, and maintained its world-wide reputation, by making us the object on which they have lavished unstinted praise and beautiful testimonials.

We accept with more than pleasure what you have presented, and will ever esteem it an honor to grace with this sword and belt our Eminent Commanders, when they preside over our Commandery, or lead it forth to join in doing honor to the Order when receiving pilgrims travelling from afar. It is our heart's desire that in all the future we, the members of Fredericksburg Commandery, Knights Templars, girded and armed by you, may stand for the name and the families and the firesides of the wives and daughters of the members of De Molay Commandery of Boston, regarding them with yourselves as members of the same household of faith — one with us in a common brotherhood. "Let brotherly love continue."

With knightly courtesy and regard we remain, your Fraters,

    EMINENT SIR R. S. CHEW, ⎫
           SIR J. W. ADAMS, ⎬ *Committee.*
           SIR R. J. McBRIDE, ⎭

From the Minutes.

Attest: WM. H. RUSSELL, *Recorder.*

WASHINGTON, D. C., April 10, 1882.

To the Officers and Members of De Molay Commandery of Knights Templars, Boston, Mass.:

Sir Knights, — We have the honor to forward herewith a slight acknowledgment of the magnificent gift presented by you to this Commandery, which we hope you will accept, not for its intrinsic value, which is but a mite as compared with your munificence, but that you may have something in your Asylum to recall to your memory, from time to time, the social pleasures mutually enjoyed by us during your sojourn in this city. Trusting that the bond of union so auspiciously begun may be cemented by time into a blissful future, and that you, like ourselves, will cherish those pleasant hours which to us appeared of too short duration, we have the honor to be, courteously and fraternally, your obedient servants,

E. F. LAWSON,
    Eminent Commander,
CHAS. L. PATTEN,
    Generalissimo,
J. H. JOCHUM,
    Captain-General.
} *Committee.*

A beautiful souvenir was received with the above letter, elegantly framed and engrossed, containing the following sentiment, under the seal of the Commandery:

DE MOLAY
MOUNTED COMMANDERY,
K.—No. 4.—T.
WASHINGTON, D. C.
TO
DE MOLAY COMMANDERY,
BOSTON, MASS.,

——— Greeting. ———

IN TOKEN OF OUR APPRECIATION OF THE PRINCELY
GIFT OF A MAGNIFICENT

EMINENT COMMANDER'S SWORD AND BELT,

PRESENTED FEBRUARY 22, 1882.

"*Hæc olim meminisse juvabit.*"

www.ingramcontent.com/pod-product-compliance
Lightning Source LLC
Chambersburg PA
CBHW030349170426
43202CB00010B/1314